Captain Blue on the Blue Blazes

Captain Blue on the Blue Blazes

The First Solo Thru-Hike of Ohio's 1,444 Mile Buckeye Trail

by Andy Niekamp

All events in this book are true. Any mistakes as to content are in no way intentional; they are products of the author's own recollection and interpretation of his experiences.

ISBN-13: 978-0-9903547-7-2

Cover photo: Hocking State Forest, Ohio by Andy Niekamp; Inset photo, Cox Media Group/*Dayton Daily News*
Interior photos: Andy Niekamp; Pages 186, 187, Cox Media Group/ *Dayton Daily News*
Cover design: Jim Murphy, Murphy & Co. Graphic Communications
Interior design: Jennifer Pinkley
Composition: Darlene Karoly
Maps: Darlene Karoly
The Buckeye Trail map and logo are used with permission from the Buckeye Trail Association.

Third Revision, March 2019

Published By:
Outdoor Adventure Connection Press
Dayton, Ohio 45439

Does the person make the journey, or does the journey make the person?

Printed in the United States of America

This book is dedicated to Karen Power for her talent,
devotion, and never-ending energy for this project.
Without her passion, this book could not have been written.

Table of Contents

Introduction

On June 15, 2011, Andy "Captain Blue" Niekamp became a hometown hero when he completed the first solo thru-hike of the 1,444 mile Buckeye Trail. His was not the first thru-hike of the Buckeye Trail, neither was it the first solo hike. A few before him had also solo hiked the trail from end-to-end. The significance of Captain Blue's accomplishment is that he is the first to complete the trail as a solo, single continuous journey at its current 1,444-mile length.

Building the Buckeye Trail to its current length was a process that took years. The trail was originally envisioned in 1958 as a 500-mile diagonal footpath that stretched from the banks of the Ohio River in Cincinnati to Conneaut on the shores of Lake Erie. The loop around the four corners of Ohio was completed in sections and finally closed by 1993. The trail continued to evolve as it was revised, rerouted, and expanded to include more off-road miles, significant landmarks, and additional historic places. In 2005, the Buckeye Trail reached its current 1,444 mile length, the longest circular trail in the U.S. to date.

When Captain Blue laced up his hiking boots and shouldered his backpack in the spring of 2011, even he wasn't sure the Buckeye Trail was a hike he wanted to complete. It's not a trail that appeals to most long-distance hikers. The challenge, but also the draw of the Buckeye Trail, is that it winds through wilderness, farmland, small towns, big cities, rural and urban areas. However, as Captain Blue re-discovered his home state on foot, a transformation began and a story took shape.

All readers will appreciate the literary theme of the hero's journey—the ordinary person who, with the nurture of community, faces obstacles and challenge after challenge until the journey transforms the hero into someone extraordinary, someone who emerges better, stronger, and wiser.

This story is about tenacity, perseverance, friendship, love, blind faith in humanity, personal resourcefulness, and a healthy dose of German stubbornness. It's a story worth reading.

I invite you on this unforgettable journey with Captain Blue. Such a journey is within the grasp of us all.

Karen "Tagalong" Power, Ph.D.
Assistant Editor, *The Antioch Review*

Preface

When I started this journey in 2011, my goal was to have fun. Fun is what has led me to log over 14,000 miles as a long-distance hiker. It works for me. What I have learned about my kind of fun is that the reward lies in the adventure. Yes, adventure—that risky endeavor filled with excitement. Adventure has become my passion.

I decided before I even began this journey that if the Buckeye Trail couldn't provide adventure, I wasn't going to commit to completing the entire 1,444 miles in a single, continuous journey. To be honest, I began this hike with a fair dose of skepticism as to how much adventure Ohio and the Buckeye Trail would provide. Perhaps if I had known that the spring of 2011 would bring enough rainfall to cause epic flooding in parts of the Midwest and one of the wettest spring seasons on record in Ohio, or that March and April temperatures would be well below normal for Ohio, I would have never attempted a spring hike.

But, hiking a 1,444 mile trail teaches you important things. One is that you can't hike the Buckeye Trail and not have an adventure. Powerful forces keep the adventure alive—the *people*, the *places*, the *past* history of Ohio, and *present*-day Ohio. It's a theme I call the *Four P's*. Ohio was suddenly new to me. My adventure was a walk through time, an up-close and firsthand encounter with present-day Ohio and Ohioans, and an exciting discovery of "Northern" hospitality.

The Buckeye Trail has changed in positive ways since 2011. My original blog raised an awareness of ways the trail could be improved. Difficult sections have become more navigable, better maintained, and blazing has improved especially in the Whipple Loop.

I expected that I would learn a lot about Ohio on this state-wide, 1,444 mile walking tour. What I didn't expect was how much I would learn about myself. This book tells a story I hope you enjoy.

Andy "Captain Blue" Niekamp
buckeyetrailhiker.com

Acknowledgments

Many people helped me with this book. I would like to express my sincere appreciation to all who read, wrote, revised, offered comments and assisted me in the editing, proofreading and design. I am especially indebted to the following:

- Karen Power for her writing talent.
- Darlene Karoly for her talent as a graphic artist.
- Jennifer Pinkley for publishing expertise.
- Janet Bolton, my mother, for giving me a lifetime of love, encouragement, and support for all of my adventures.
- To all of the people on my Buckeye Trail hike who assisted me along the way.
- The Buckeye Trail Association for graphics and historical information.

My spirit finally broke. Hiking the trail in this condition was too tough on me. I realized that I wasn't hiking the trail. I was fighting the trail instead. I came to the Buckeye Trail to hike it, not fight it.

BUCKEYE TRAIL
EST. 1959
DEFIANCE
PEMBERVILLE
NORWALK
MEDINA
BEDFORD
BURTON
AKRON
MOGADORE
MASSILLON
BOWERSTON
BELLE VALLEY
ROAD FORK
WHIPPLE
STOCKPORT
NEW STRAITSVILLE
OLD MAN'S CAVE
SCIOTO TRAIL
SINKING SPRING
SHAWNEE
WEST UNION
WILLIAMSBURG
LOVELAND
CAESAR CREEK
TROY
ST. MARYS
DELPHOS

CHAPTER 1
The Call to Adventure

February 24, 2011
The Idea Moves Forward

I'm an Ohio boy from Kettering, a suburb of Dayton, who likes to hike long distances. It all began . . . well mostly began . . . in 1989 when I hiked 35 miles on the Appalachian Trail (AT) in the Great Smoky Mountains National Park. I got whupped by the trail and hooked at the same time.

I returned the next year to walk all 70 miles of the Appalachian Trail in the Great Smokies and then 105 miles in Shenandoah National Park. I've been hiking continuous, multi-day journeys ever since. Just a few months ago, I completed the 2,179-mile Appalachian Trail, end-to-end, for the third time. Only 30 other people besides me have successfully reported hiking the entire AT three times.

At the moment, I'm in Orange Beach, Alabama, a resort town with spectacular beach front on the Gulf of Mexico. I've been migrating here for a month-long hiatus every winter since 2008. I drive down to escape the Ohio winter and to plan hiking trips for the year. I'm itching to plan a new adventure.

Wilderness trails appeal to me. It's nature up close and personal. There are no wilderness trails in Ohio, so I've never done much backpacking in my home state. However, it's not for lack of long-distance trails. Many trails traverse Ohio: the North Country Trail, the American

Discovery Trail, the North Coast Inland Trail, and a very, very long circular trail around the state called the Buckeye Trail.

The Buckeye Trail has a unique appeal because it's exclusive to Ohio. Most hikers chip away at the 1,444 miles of trail by walking in short sections. That takes a very long time. Some folks I know have been hiking the Buckeye Trail for years. It dawned on me during one of my morning walks on the beach that if I hiked the trail in a single, continuous journey, I could complete a thru-hike of the Buckeye Trail in just a matter of a few months.

The time seems right. The Buckeye Trail Association Trail Talk discussion board recently debuted. The discussion board is a place where Buckeye Trail hikers can connect. Hikers ask questions, share information, and give advice. Reading other hikers' comments and questions planted the seed that a thru-hike might be do-able. The more I thought about hiking the 1,444 miles of the Buckeye Trail in a single journey, the more I was drawn to the idea. However, it's a difficult trail to thru-hike. Few have done it since the trail was completed as a closed circuit loop. I would be only the sixth person to thru-hike it.

Maybe it's time to try something new—something out of my comfort zone. Yes, the Buckeye Trail appeals to me, but (and I have big "buts"), I'll be a fish out of water. The Buckeye Trail is a different hiking experience. It winds through big cities, small towns, suburbs, and countryside with only parts in forests. I'll be a pedestrian doing miles of road walking. Plus the biggest unknown to a Buckeye Trail thru-hiker is where to sleep. Campgrounds or other predictable places to stay are not common like they are on the Appalachian Trail. However, a long-distance hiker knows that it's impossible to plan every detail of a long, continuous journey. I'll have to figure lodging out one day at a time.

This urban, suburban, rural journey may not be for me. I may abandon it after three days or three weeks. I just don't know.

For the time being, I'm putting second thoughts aside. I'm ready to take the first step. I have cleared my calendar of obligations for 12 weeks and ordered the complete set of 26 maps, one for each Buckeye Trail circuit section. I'll stay on trail for as long as it's fun.

Laissez les bons temps rouler! (*Let the good times roll!*)

March 9
Selecting My Start Date

The start date of my Buckeye Trail hike is Sunday, March 20, 2011. There is no real significance to this date other than it's the first day of spring, and I'm anxious to get hiking.

I made the decision today to keep a record of this journey by blogging in real time. I post regularly on Facebook when I'm hiking because friends and family seem to like following my journeys. However, I've never blogged before. I don't know if I'll be any good at it or not.

Compared to Facebook, though, blogging is a better mechanism to capture daily events. It's easy with the free blogger software that's available. I don't have to go to a computer in a library. I can just sit in my tent with my smartphone, write about my day, and publish. It'll be slow going because I'm literally all thumbs when I type on my phone, but it's do-able. I'll blog as part of my daily hiking routine. My mom is a retired English teacher, so I'll do my best to make her proud of my writing skills.

I have just 20 days to plan my hike. It's not much time for such a long hike.

March 14
One Week to Go!

The start of my hike is just one week away. I'm mostly ready. I'm packing my standard Appalachian Trail gear with a couple of exceptions. My backpacking equipment includes a tent, sleeping bag, two sleeping pads, alcohol stove, small pot, hiking poles, rain gear, warm clothes, maps, compass, pocket knife, cell phone, and toiletries. I've packed winter and summer gear, but I'll figure out what I really need along the way and acquire it or mail home what I don't need.

What I'm not carrying and what adds a lot of weight is food. It feels weird not to have a large pile of food ready to be packed into resupply boxes as I normally do for an Appalachian Trail hike. My plan is to resupply along the way and eat in restaurants when convenient. I'm trusting the advice that food is readily available along the Buckeye

My fully loaded backpack has everything I need to live outside

Trail. The good news is that the space I save by not bringing packaged food, I'll use for extra clothes.

I have friends and family who live within a 60-mile radius of Dayton. So, for the first four nights of my journey, I've made arrangements to stay with people I know. I'll get picked up at the end of my hiking day and sleep comfortably out of the elements. I don't know where I'll sleep the fifth night or any night after that. Hopefully, I can find suitable camping sites.

March 19
One Day to Go!

As usual, there is still a lot to do. I have all the major tasks covered, but the list of small chores to take care of seems endless. Some just won't get done. In the long run, it won't matter.

My fully loaded pack weighs 29 pounds, plus about three pounds of water. This is way too heavy! I need to find some items to take out. This will be a task for tomorrow morning.

So far the weather for the next few days looks like a typical March in Ohio. Rain and cold are in the forecast.

As usual, I have the standard pre-hike anxiety. I'm blocking self-doubt as best I can, but the reality is that planning a long-distance hike is easier said than done. At some point, the planning stops and the journey begins. I woke up last night thinking, *whoa, am I really gonna do this? A 1,444-mile hike? It's here. It's time. It's time to take that first step. Did I prepare properly? Do I know what I'm doing? Is this even a realistic expectation?* Self-doubt was creeping in.

I have other doubts, too. I enjoy the challenge and the adventure—the element of the unknown and the unexpected. But would I find the same adventure on the Buckeye Trail that a wilderness hike brings? Hiking 1,444 miles around Ohio surely would be an adventure, wouldn't it? I was born in Ohio; I was raised in Ohio; I went to school in Ohio; I went to college in Ohio; I worked in Ohio, and Ohio is boring. Believe me, Ohio is not exciting. How could this be a great journey when Ohio is so boring?

Then, there are the usual challenges. I'm physically and mentally strong and have often called hiking "my personal fountain of youth," but hikers are unprotected from the elements. The Ohio spring weather can be rainy, windy, hot, humid, and cold all in the same day. Plus, the exposure to the environment is unpredictable. I'm carrying only a small pocket knife and my phone for emergencies.

I thrive on the feeling of independence and self-reliance I experience on the trail, but I don't have it all figured out. I don't know how things are going to unfold, and what I'm going to encounter. It's impossible to be prepared for everything that may happen. Ready or not, tomorrow is go day.

BUCKEYE
EST. 1959
TRAIL

CHAPTER 2
The Adventure Begins

March 20: Day 1
The Stranger Smiled and Extended His Hand

I hiked 18 miles to Tipp City.

My hike on the Buckeye Trail started at 10:30 a.m. on a chilly but sunny Sunday morning at Deeds Point MetroPark in Dayton to the sound of ringing church bells. Today is the first day of spring.

The Buckeye Trail is a circular trail, so technically, there is no definitive start point or end point. Some hikers start at either the northern terminus at Headlands Beach State Park on the shore of Lake Erie or at the southern terminus in Eden Park, Cincinnati. Since the Buckeye Trail passes through Dayton, the "Outdoor Adventure Capital of the Midwest," I chose to start from home. I was dropped off by my mother and her husband, Jim, at Deeds Point downtown.

It seemed appropriate to begin my adventure in the presence of Dayton's most famous adventurers. Life-size statues of Wilbur and Orville Wright stand at Deeds Point. I posed for the obligatory photo with the Wright brothers. My mom gave me a hug and asked when I'd be home again. I just shook my head and gave her the best answer I had, "I don't know." I've set my expectations for completing the Buckeye Trail really low and have avoided making any grand announcements to friends and family just in case I decide to abandon this adventure before it even gets started. I waved goodbye and starting walking north.

Captain Blue at Deeds Point MetroPark, downtown Dayton

It felt good to be "on trail." It's an expression long-distance hikers use to announce the start of a trip. The sunny day turned warm. I saw lots of people riding bikes and walking on the bike path along the Great Miami River. Immediately, I was struck with the feeling that I'm out of place. On the Appalachian Trail, hikers are a common sight. A fellow with hiking poles on a bike trail in an urban area wearing a backpack and hiker clothes, however, is like waving a sign saying "homeless" or "dangerous stranger."

Several people I passed refused to make eye contact with me, and a few others suddenly felt the urge to make a cell phone call when they saw me coming. I felt awkward. Just when I thought I'd have to get used to dirty looks, a stranger struck up a conversation with me. He was different from anyone I had seen on the path that day. I could tell by his body language that he wanted to talk to me, that he wasn't afraid of me. He asked what I was doing.

"I'm Andy, and I'm hiking the Buckeye Trail." I handed him a self-designed (a.k.a. "homemade") business card. The card has the Buckeye Trail logo on it, my trail name, my real name, my e-mail address, and the website address of my blog. The card is a way to introduce myself. I also want people to know that I'm a hiker on a journey around Ohio. I hoped that this stranger would be impressed.

"Lee Kreider," the stranger smiled and extended his hand.

It turns out, I was the one impressed. I stood there amazed as Lee told me the story of how that path on which we were standing came to be. He was active in the Buckeye Trail Association about 40 years ago when there was no Buckeye Trail through Dayton. It was Lee, and his friend, Woody Ensor, who were instrumental in persuading the board to extend the trail from Cincinnati northward through Dayton to northwest Ohio. The board was skeptical of building a trail through a major city and thought that western Ohio was too boring. Members wanted to route the Buckeye Trail through the Bellefontaine highlands. It was Lee who sold the board on the idea that the canal corridor through west central and north central Ohio offered the "highway" they were looking for. His idea landed him an appointment on the board of trustees where he became instrumental in creating what became the Buckeye Trail and later, the Great Miami River bike path.

I could hardly contain my excitement. I had just crossed paths with the man who pioneered the path I was traveling! I felt a sudden surge of confidence. Lee gave me something to be happy about. He gave me something to cling to that first critical day of my hike when I wasn't sure if I'd be able to stick with it. He made me feel good about what I was doing. He didn't offer help in the traditional way that locals help hikers. He didn't offer me a candy bar; he didn't offer to give me a ride; he offered emotional support. It was the best gift I could have received. What an amazing and much appreciated coincidence!

P.S. I got my pack weight down to 26 pounds!

March 21: Day 2
History in My Own Backyard

It was a 17-mile day into Piqua.

It stormed last night. Lots of lightning and thunder. I was glad I was indoors and not in a tent. My friend Diane Brown plucked me off the trail in Tipp City yesterday. She had a wonderful meal waiting for me and let me stay the night. I was back on trail early this morning.

My feet were sore from walking on miles of paved surfaces yesterday, and today's walk was mostly pavement. Still, it was a lovely morning for walking. The birds were chirping and spring was in the air.

The Buckeye Trail in Taylorsville MetroPark follows a short stretch on canal towpath. Tadmor, which is along the path, is the remnant of a booming canal town. Locals say it's haunted. Abandoned after the Great Dayton Flood of 1913, some claim during a full moon, the sound of horses and the voices of canal boat operators can still be heard.

I made good time as I strolled through neighborhoods, passed factories, businesses, schools, municipal buildings, and the county courthouse in Troy. I even walked along the Great Miami River. This trail variety is what makes the Buckeye Trail so unique. I took a break at Tim Horton's in Troy. A lady asked me if I was that guy who was walking across the country. I told her no, just Ohio. I hope she wasn't disappointed.

As I approached Piqua, I was surprised to learn that it was once known worldwide as "the Atomic City." A nuclear reactor was built as an experiment to test the viability of harnessing atomic energy to

Waterfall on creek, Piqua

produce electricity. It operated for a few years during the 1960s and then was shut down. It sits right next to the Buckeye Trail along the Great Miami River.

I couldn't believe I was standing in front of the first nuclear station in the United States to produce electricity for a city. How is it that I grew up in Dayton and never knew there was a nuclear power plant in my own backyard and that it was the first of its kind in the nation? For the second day in a row, I had a reason to feel good about what I was doing. I'm going to see things that I would have never seen from a car window, things I can only experience by walking.

P.S. I developed a small blister on my left heel. Bummer.

March 22: Day 3
60 Seconds of My Time Well Spent

I hiked 20 miles and finished in Newport.

I spent last night and will spend tonight with my friend, Rick Thien, in Minster. He is a bachelor like me and lives by himself. Rick dropped me off in downtown Piqua early this morning on his way to work.

I'm slackpacking today. A slackpack is carrying only what a hiker needs for the day. So, I took out my tent and camping gear which lightened my pack by 10 pounds. Today will be mainly road walking.

It did not take long for my feet to hurt. Walking on pavement is hard on my feet. A road to the normal eye looks flat, but it isn't. Asphalt roads are designed so that the high point is the middle of the road, sloping down on either side to allow for rain runoff. As I face traffic, my left leg is constantly hitting the pavement just a few millimeters lower than my right leg due to the roadway's crown. I can feel pain in my left foot. I can also feel pain in my left thigh. I also developed a soreness in my ankle because I'm not walking on a level surface. Every step is painful. I wonder how long it will take my thighs, calves, feet and ankles to adjust to this new normal.

The highlight of my day was a fellow in a truck who stopped me to ask what I was doing. He had seen me earlier in the day while driving a school bus. He saw me again, still walking, and was curious. I gave him one of my business cards. It seems that many people in Ohio, even native-born and raised Ohioans, have never heard of the Buckeye Trail

Lockington Dam Reserve, Lockington

or that it visits 44 of Ohio's 88 counties, or that the first few miles were dedicated as a state-wide trail system 52 years ago, or that it is now 1,444 miles long, the longest loop trail in the nation. So, the very first introduction many people are going to have to the Buckeye Trail is me. I see myself as an ambassador for the Buckeye Trail. I also hope people will follow my progress by reading my blog. The friendly truck driver seemed truly surprised to learn about the Buckeye Trail. It was 60 seconds of my time well spent.

I came across an Appalachian Trail-style overnight shelter along the Buckeye Trail. It wasn't listed on the map. By the way, here's something interesting about Buckeye Trail maps—they are very unique, not like any map I've ever used before in my entire hiking experience.

I'll explain. The Buckeye Trail is 1,444 miles long and is divided into 26 sections. There's one map for each section, hence, 26 maps. Each section is about 45–70 miles in length. Each section map includes a small geographical map and further divides the section into 25–30 points. Each point has a written description that gives cardinal directions, road names, landmarks, history, and any other information that the designers thought would be helpful or interesting, all on a piece of map-quality paper folded into a small square the size of a shirt pocket.

Most of the time, the map directions don't make a lot of sense until the exact moment when a hiker comes to the location that is being described. So, the hiker not only needs to follow the blue blazes, but also frequently thumb the map. The reason is practical. If the map says, "After 0.4 mi at primitive crossroads, pass a sign that warns of use by automobile from here N to Dye Rd. Continue N past house (360′). After 0.5 mi, pass both a sign for the Ross Family Homestead (1940–2002) and decrepit artifacts from Lock 13" as it does on the Troy section map, the hiker needs to pay close attention to avoid missing a turn, which is never welcomed or enjoyable.

March 23: Day 4
Adventure is in my Blood

I took a zero day in Minster.

My friend Rick has graciously invited me to stay another day at his house in Minster. Today is my first "zero day." That's a zero-mile day. Translation: No hiking. My feet are killing me. After three days and 55 miles of mostly pavement walking, I need to give my sore feet a break.

I usually take a zero day after seven or ten days. But after three days of flat hiking and battling cold and wind, I'm ready, and I'm in a good place to do it. It's raining today. Rick is letting me use his car while he is at work. So, I took the opportunity to visit family graves—my four grandparents and my father.

Minster is a very familiar place to me. My family heritage is rooted here. Both of my parents grew up near here. My trail name is Captain Blue. My birth name is Andrew J. Niekamp, III. My family on both sides—the Willkes and the Niekamps—were immigrants who came to this part of Ohio from Germany.

They arrived via the Miami & Erie Canal in the 1830s, settling in wilderness where the American Indians had been driven out only a few years earlier. They were farmers back in Germany, so it was natural that they purchased cheap land from the government, cleared it, and became farmers.

Germans thrived in communities and owned banks, grocery stores, newspapers, churches, cemeteries, and schools. Lots of the towns in this area have German names—Minster, New Bremen, Ottoville. My grandparents, the Willkes, are buried in Maria Stein which means "Mary of the Rock" in German. My father and my Grandpa and Grandma Niekamp are buried in St. Henry, just down the road.

Grandma Willke wrote extensive family history. She was proud of her heritage and wanted us to be proud of it too. As the family story goes, life in Germany was hard and my ancestors were looking for a better life. My maternal great, great grandparents arrived in America with only the clothes they were wearing and $1 they received from a sponsor. They worked hard and were eventually able to buy land.

They continued to speak German. My grandma writes, "As a child, I spoke low German. When I started school, I learned to read and write in German as well as English. My first reader was in German, and we learned English through translations. During World War I, it was considered pro-German to teach German in the schools, so, it was discontinued. I was probably in the 5th grade then."

Most, but not all, of my German ancestors were farmers. My great-grandfather Willke moved to Maria Stein in 1893 where he opened a medical practice. Since that time, six family members over the last 118 years have become doctors and practiced in the area. The family practice in Maria Stein continues to this day.

It feels right to be doing this hike. I come from a family of adventurers. My ancestors were willing to leave everything behind and proceed with uncertainty to do something new, different, and dangerous. My family members who made the long voyage to America were the ones who were willing to risk everything to start a new life, a better life. I deeply admire them, and am proud to be one of them. Adventure is in my blood.

March 24: Day 5
A Big German Catholic Family

I hiked 19 miles to St. Marys.

Rick dropped me off in Newport at 7:45 a.m. Hiking today was almost entirely along the Miami & Erie Canal tow path with the exception of

2.5 miles on the road. Northwest Ohio is flat farm country—a topography sculpted by the glaciers. It's field after field as far as I could see. The road walking was quite chilly and overcast with nothing to stop the brisk north wind.

A light coat of snow covered parts of the ground. Cold weather is good for hiking when trying to lay down miles. There's less motivation to dilly-dally or take breaks. Today was my first "twelve by twelve." Translation: hiking 12 miles by 12 noon.

I stopped in New Bremen for a break. The Buckeye Trail goes through downtown New Bremen because the Miami & Erie Canal went right through New Bremen. New Bremen's claim to topographical fame is that it's the farthest point south on the North American continent where the water flows north. From here water flows nearly 700 miles north through the St. Lawrence Seaway to the Atlantic Ocean.

New Bremen marks the end of the 19-mile stretch of the Loramie Summit. The summit is the highest point between the Ohio River in Cincinnati and Lake Erie in Toledo. South of the summit, the canal water flows to Cincinnati. North of the summit, the canal water flows to Toledo. I climbed roughly 200 feet in elevation from Dayton. Technically speaking, I will be hiking downhill about 400 feet to Lake Erie from here.

The Miami & Erie Canal locks are numbered relative to this feature. New Bremen is Lock 1 North because it's the first lock going north from the highest point. Going south from the Loramie Summit, is Lock 1 South. Numbering didn't start at the end points—Cincinnati or Toledo. It began here from the summit where New Bremen is.

I took a brief tour of the reconstructed lock tender's house at Lock 1 North. The job of the lock tender was to raise and lower the water level as he took canal boats through the lock. Today, it houses the New Bremen Chamber of Commerce and has interesting facts about canal history.

By 3:45 p.m., I arrived at the Buckeye Trail crossing at SR-219 just south of St. Marys. My first cousin, Tom Rammel, lives just a mile from the trail. I will spend the next two nights with Tom. Tom is just one of my dozens of first cousins. Yes, dozens.

Here's a brief Niekamp family tree synopsis. I come from a big German Catholic family. I am the oldest son of five kids. My father had eight siblings and my mother, three. The Catholic tradition of natural family planning has yielded almost 70 first cousins, with 55 grandchildren on my father's side and 19 on my mother's. What's really cool is that many family members still live in this area. Tom and I are the same age and have always enjoyed hanging around each other. I look forward to catching up on family news.

March 25: Day 6
A Headless Man on the Bridge at Night

I hiked 17 miles to Spencerville.

The canal was an important transportation corridor which moved farm products out of the wilderness and into cities where farmers could fetch a higher price. Not only did agricultural products make it to the big cities, but goods from the cities then made it to these rural areas. Spencerville and towns along the Buckeye Trail in this area sprung up along the Miami & Erie route. My route today was entirely on the canal towpath and filled with vestiges of canal history.

Lock 8 North is my favorite. It's a majestic relic in the middle of farm country that I call the "forgotten giant" because it's big—16′ deep and 90′ long—and because most people don't know it's here. It has not been restored like Lock 1 in New Bremen and is not visible from the road. It's in good shape probably because its walls are stone, not wood like some other locks. The individual stones probably weigh a ton or two. I can picture the mules tethered to a canal boat guided by the mule driver slowly pulling into the lock. The divots in the stone made by the heavy hemp rope are still visible.

Building the canals was a task of monumental proportions. Before Ohio was settled by whites, 90–95% was forest land. The wilderness was so thick that it was said that a (fairly ambitious) squirrel could travel across the state on treetops alone.

As difficult as it was for the canals to be built and as long as the project took to complete, canals lost their usefulness for two reasons. First, railroads that had arrived in the 1830s could operate all year round. The water in the canals froze during the winter. They made nice ice rinks for locals but were no use for travel. The second contributing factor to the demise of the canals was the 1913 Great Ohio Flood. Many canal locks were damaged beyond repair. History would say, however, that the canal corridor served its purpose. And today, other major transportation corridors like the CSX railroad line and I-75 parallel its course.

The canal brought drama, too. Bloody Bridge was the scene of a double homicide when two canal boat workers fell in love with the same girl. The bronze marker at the scene of the crime reads:

> During the canal years of the 1850's, a rivalry grew between Bill Jones and Jack Billings for the love of Minnie Warren. There became hatred by Bill because Minnie chose Jack. On a fall night in 1854, returning from a party, Minnie and Jack were surprised on the bridge by Bill, armed with an axe. With one swing, Bill severed Jack's head. Seeing this, Minnie screamed and fell into a watery grave. Bill disappeared, and when a skeleton was found years later in a nearby well, people asked was it suicide or justice?

Some say the bridge is haunted. One legend tells of a headless man who can sometimes be seen on the bridge at night. Another says that

Lock 8 North on the Miami & Erie Canal, St. Marys

Minnie Warren's face can be seen on moonlit nights in the dark water. The Buckeye Trail passes Bloody Bridge, and Minnie is believed to be buried in an unmarked grave just down the road. I was glad I was not there at night!

Just beyond Bloody Bridge is the stone aqueduct over Six-Mile Creek. The canal had to cut across many creeks and rivers. Aqueducts were built to elevate the canal over these bodies of water. The Miami & Erie Canal has 19 aqueducts. This aqueduct is still in remarkably good shape.

Around 3:30 p.m., I strolled into Spencerville. My cousin arrived a few minutes later and took me back to St. Marys for the night.

March 26: Day 7
"Captain Blue" Has Stuck Ever Since

I hiked 20 miles to Ottoville.

It was a cold and windy day. The temperature was in the 20s with a 10–15 mile sustained wind that lasted all day. In this flat farm country, there is not much to block the wind. I layered up to trap body heat under my outer shell, and I also wore a hat and gloves. I was bundled up and warm.

Ottoville was founded in 1845. Father John Otto Bredeick, a Catholic priest, brought a group of Germans here from Prussia to escape religious persecution. A beautiful, large Gothic, twin-steepled church with stained glass windows in town is a reminder of the religious heritage on which Ottoville was founded.

The church sits just outside the perimeter of the "Land of the Cross-Tipped Churches," a National Register historic site. Thirty-six Catholic churches were built in the 19th and 20th centuries within a 22-mile radius around Maria Stein. I walked through this area on the Buckeye Trail just two days ago. It's possible on a clear day to see as many as seven church steeples off in the distance.

The first nine miles to Delphos were on the canal tow path. The canal tow path makes for enjoyable hiking because the trail is so well blazed. No need to stay focused on navigating. The rectangular 2″ x 6″ Sherwin Williams Sweeping Blue #2408 blazes are supposed to be visible at eye level, but sometimes they're hard to spot. Blazes fade over

Immaculate Conception Church, Ottoville

time, but sometimes there may not be a suitable spot to paint a blaze or sometimes landowners don't want hikers coming through their property, so they purposefully cover the blazes. I even know of a few cities unwilling to allow public property to be blazed.

In these cases, trail maintainers need to get creative. I've seen blazes on utility poles, power line towers, fence posts, highway guard rails, pavement, trees, fallen trees, rocks, and any structural variation of the former. I had trouble getting out of Piqua a few days ago because I couldn't find the blazes. I had to rely on joggers and pedestrians to direct me out of town. Today though, no scavenger hunts looking for blazes.

At a road crossing just before Delphos, a fellow in a pick-up truck, Sam Bonifas, stopped and asked "Are you Captain Blue?" Turns out, Sam is an Ohio State Parks volunteer who lives in this area and was reading my daily blog. I knew he was a fellow hiker because he called me by my trail name.

This is a good spot to explain my trail name. A trail name is a special moniker bestowed upon a hiker. A trail name is a way to self-identify and also to differentiate one hiker from other hikers. A trail name can be adopted in various, usually creative, ways. It can be a characteristic (like "Chatter Box"), a person's profession (like "Professor"), or something stupid a hiker does (like "Flash" for catching a camp stove on fire). It's also a way to remain anonymous. I heard of a guy who embezzled money from his employer and lived happily for two years on the AT under the alias of his trail name.

My trail name was born one night in 1994 in north Georgia at an Appalachian Trail shelter. On this particular trip, I happened to be wearing a lot of blue—blue long underwear, blue fleece shirt. It was a cool evening so I had on a blue hat, gloves, and blue socks. My buddies started calling me *Blueberry.*

It's best if the hiker picks the name. If other hikers pick it, it may not be very flattering. "Blueberry" was not flattering. But after five years as a long-distance hiker, it was time to pick a trail name. So I said, "Shorten it to 'Blue.'" Then I thought about it for a minute and said, "Just call me 'Captain Blue.'" *Captain* was a nickname given to me by my caving buddies years ago who said it suited me. Maybe it does. Being the oldest of four boys—a.k.a., the instigator/facilitator/supervisor of activities that we hoped Mom wouldn't find out about—probably perfected my captain-like qualities. "Captain-like," yes, but not in the austere military sense, more like an adventure-seeking, free-spirited pirate sense. Anyway, Captain Blue has stuck ever since.

I am spending tonight again in St. Marys. I am pleased to see that my picture is in the St. Marys newspaper today. Yesterday, a well-dressed gentleman spotted me in Memorial Park in St. Marys. Turns out, he is the law director for the city. He asked lots of questions about my journey. Then he walked me across the street to the offices of the *St. Marys Leader* for a picture. Only seven days on the trail, and I made front-page local news. Woot! Woot! The first time I ever made the news as a hiker was just last year when I gave a presentation at Minster Middle School about hiking the Appalachian Trail. I'm happy St. Marys considers hikers newsworthy or maybe someone at the paper found out my cousin Tom works for the city. Anyway, front page is a first for me!

BUCKEYE
EST. 1959
TRAIL

CHAPTER 3
First Encounters

March 27: Day 8
The Sign Read "No Trespassing"

I walked 17 miles from Charloe back to Ottoville.

My cousin Tom dropped me off today in Charloe, the site of a former Ottowa Indian village. I hiked from Charloe southbound to Ottoville or counter-clockwise as the map calls it.

My hike this morning began on the banks of the Auglaize River. The Auglaize River flows north to the Maumee River. I soon reached the confluence of the Auglaize River and the Little Auglaize River where Fort Brown once stood. Fort Brown was a wooden stockade fort used during the War of 1812. It was built by either General William Henry Harrison or Colonel Brown, depending on which of the two historical bronze markers is true (or maybe the colonel built the fort and the general took the credit). The fort was used in the campaign against the British and the Indians. Today nothing remains, just the flags to indicate where it once stood. I stood at the spot to absorb the moment. I wondered if the sight of these two majestic, rolling rivers merging into one great waterway inspired pride and courage in the soldiers who defended our young nation.

For the first time on this hike, I stood in front of a sign that read, "No Trespassing." It was located where the trail leaves the road and follows the canal through woods. Two small boards were nailed over the blue blazes that were meant to tell a hiker that the trail turns from the road onto a path through the woods. The boards were hiding the blazes so hikers would not see them.

Was I on state-owned land or private land? Apparently, the adjacent land owner believed he or she had rights to the canal towpath and wanted hikers to keep out. I double checked the route with my map. The map indicated that the land owner was wrong. I took the boards down. Whoever put the boards up is not going to be happy. I wondered who or what else would try to block my path on this journey.

At 6:15 p.m., I strolled into Ottoville. My Uncle Don was there waiting for me. He drove me back to St. Marys. It may seem odd that I started from the north today and hiked south instead of hiking a steady northern direction like I've done for the past eight days.

In hiking terms, it's called a "flip-flop." There are practical reasons for flip-flopping. One reason is that hikers rely on friends, taxis, or even strangers to shuttle them to and from the trail head. It was more convenient for today's shuttle driver, my Uncle Don Schwieterman, to pick me up in Ottoville. He dropped me at Tom's house in St. Marys for the night because Tom decided that it was best if I stayed another night at his house instead of camping. It is too cold and windy for him to let his cousin spend a night outside. I agreed. It will be nice to be inside again during this cold snap.

After tonight, I'll be out of range for daily shuttles back and forth from the trail to Tom's house. Spending the last three days at Tom's house allowed me to slackpack. I made good time by carrying only what I needed for each day. It helped bring my hike total to 128 miles. Not bad for eight days with one zero. Tomorrow I resume hiking with a full pack. I need to figure out where to sleep tomorrow night.

March 28: Day 9
Today was Literally Shocking

It was a 15-mile day to Defiance.

Paul Rammel, Tom's son, dropped me off in Charloe at 10:30 a.m. I resumed hiking with a fully loaded pack.

The next part of my day was shocking, literally. Most of the trail miles today were on roads, but a few of the miles were along the canal tow path. A farmer had erected a fence over the Buckeye Trail along a portion of the canal tow path. I didn't realize it was an electric fence until it was too late. When I straddled the fence, I felt the surge of electricity on my inner thigh. It was quite jolting. Instinctively, I dove head first to the ground to clear the fence. I landed on my shoulder and rolled. I was unhurt, but shaken.

Then I realized that in order to get out of the enclosure, I would have to climb the electric fence again. Another concern followed fast. Was the fence to keep hikers out or something in? In all likelihood, it was to keep livestock in. More than once an angry bull has chased trespassers off of private farmland. I didn't want to be one of them. So, I wandered toward the farmhouse looking for a way out. I found the pasture gate, climbed over and got back on the Buckeye Trail.

It's possible that the farmer erected the fence to claim the canal tow path land as his and wants to keep hikers out. This is the second instance of encroachment by landowners on a canal tow path that I've experienced. I was feeling frustrated with the land owner, and if I had seen that person today, I would have had some strong words about taking adverse possession of state property, the danger to hikers, and the legal liability.

The landowner is not necessarily to blame. The Buckeye Trail traverses federal, state, county and city-owned lands and some private property. In the 1800s, the state started selling off the land to private individuals surrounding the canal corridor to fund its construction. Mostly, the land was sold with easement to protect the corridor, but in a few cases, it wasn't. Villages, towns, farms, and homes grew up on either side of the corridor.

After the Great Dayton Flood of 1913, due to the subsequent catastrophic damage to the locks, and as the popularity of the railroad rose, canals were abandoned. Over the last 150 years, large portions of canal land were neglected by the state. Easement or no easement, I guess it's natural for landowners to feel that they, and not the state, own the land. Today, the Ohio Department of Natural Resources, Division of Water oversees the canal lands.

I e-mailed the Buckeye Trail Association about the incident. The trustees are well aware of areas in dispute, but have no legal power to force landowners to withdraw from state property. Even though the canal corridor has belonged to the state since the 1800s, the Ohio Department of Natural Resources prefers a gentler approach, choosing to educate rather than enforce.

I arrived in Defiance around 4:00 p.m. I explored the park at the confluence of the Maumee River and Auglaize Rivers. This is the site of Fort Defiance which was built in 1794 under orders from General "Mad" (as in "hot-tempered") Anthony Wayne to protect settlers from the Indians. It was a base of operations in the Battle of Fallen Timbers and also used during the War of 1812 against the British. In its day, it was a way-point for settlers who ventured West.

I am spending the night with my first trail angels. A trail angel is a person who performs an unexpected act of kindness for a hiker. Bill and Angie aren't family or friends. They are strangers I had met by pure chance twice just a few months prior on hiking trails in Dayton. I remembered that they lived in Defiance. It turns out that they've been trail angels in the past for other long-distance hikers. They plucked me off the trail today and tomorrow will plop me back on it. They gave me a nice meal, a shower, a bed, and use of their washer and dryer. To my great surprise (and pleasure), they even contacted the *Crescent News*, the local Defiance paper. For the second time on this journey, I've made the local news.

March 29: Day 10
Being Alone is not the Same as Being Lonely

I hiked 21 miles to a few miles outside of Napoleon.

The trail today was on soil foot path entirely along the Maumee River except for the towns of Defiance and Napoleon where I walked on roads. The Maumee River is quite wide and beautiful. The trail went through Independence Dam State Park.

I haven't seen many people on the trail. On a long-distance solo hike, there's a lot of solitude. Some people think that's a disadvantage for the solo hiker because too much alone time makes a person lonely.

Being alone is not the same as being lonely. Loneliness is an empty feeling. I'm not lonely, but I do miss seeing other people. The weather has been rainy and cold, miserable weather to be outside. Even people who like to walk tend to skip their daily walks on days like this to stay inside.

Campsite along the Maumee River near Napoleon

But today I met Denise. I spotted her off in the distance taking a walk on the canal tow path. Despite the 26-pound pack on my back, I stepped up my pace and quickly caught up with her. I was so happy to see somebody else out here, I just wanted to say, "Hey, how ya doin'?" She was friendly, and it was nice chatting with her even if it was just for a few minutes.

One overlooked advantage of solo hiking is that it's easier to meet people. People in groups tend to keep to themselves. The paradox of the solo hiker is that, if a hiker is open to it, there are more opportunities for interesting people encounters. For me, people encounters make the journey memorable.

I took a break in Florida. Florida, Ohio that is. Florida is located at approximately the midpoint between Defiance and Napoleon on the Maumee River, on what is believed to be the site of a former Native American village called Snaketown. History has it that Captain Snake, a Shawnee Indian Chief, liked to fish and camp here. Snaketown stuck as a name long after the Indians left because locals hoped it would discourage newcomers. Today, it's a town of only 232 people; maybe the name was changed to Florida for the opposite reason.

I was able to get a copy the *Defiance Crescent News* article and photo of me today all the way here in Florida!

Today is important. I have hiked over 150 miles, which means I have completed one-tenth of the Buckeye Trail. One tenth doesn't sound like much compared to the 1,294 miles I have left to go, but it's progress, and I feel happy about it.

Plus I am now starting to hike eastward instead of straight north. It has been said that spring travels northward at 15 miles per day. I've been hiking ahead of spring since I started this hike. I'm anxiously awaiting its arrival, but I see no signs. The grass isn't getting greener, the plants aren't growing, the leaves aren't coming out on the trees, the flowers that follow the daffodils haven't sprouted. The tulips aren't there. Now as I head east, spring will have a chance to catch up with me.

March 30: Day 11
Today I was "That Guy"

I walked 27 miles to Haskins.

Last night was the first night in my tent. Spending the last nine nights in the warmth of a home was a privilege, but I was itching to camp. Camping solo allows my body to set its own schedule—sleep when I'm tired and wake up when I'm rested.

I found an excellent site on a bluff overlooking the Maumee River. I pitched my tent east so I could catch the first light of sunrise. It was a cold morning with temperatures in the 20s. My boots froze; my water bottle froze. A hot cup of coffee hit the spot as I sat by the river and watched the sun come up. It was a beautiful orange. The sunshine lasted only briefly. The sun slipped quickly behind the clouds. I didn't see it the rest of the day.

The trail from Grand Rapids, Ohio to Waterville is along the tow path. It's not far from the location of the 1794 Battle of Fallen Timbers, named because it was fought in a field of trees uprooted by a tornado. There, General "Mad" Anthony Wayne defeated an alliance of Indian tribes who were fighting for control of the Northwest Territory. The entire battle lasted only 25 minutes.

The Midwest has quite a fascination with General Wayne who was well known in Ohio, Indiana, Michigan, and Pennsylvania as a

Revolutionary hero, politician, and commander over United States army forces in the Northwest Indian War. Today, over 100 cities, counties, towns, villages, schools, colleges, school districts, hotels, hospitals, businesses, highways and forests or parks bear his name, including Wayne National Forest. Today I'm hiking the Anthony Wayne Trail (US Route 24).

Route 24 is constructed on an old canal bed, which was filled with dirt and repurposed in the 1930s–1940s as US-24. The section map says US-24 is busy, dangerous, noisy, and generally unpleasant. It was right. The good news is that I only had to walk on US-24 for three miles. There are plans to move the Buckeye Trail completely off of US-24.

I stopped at a diner at the Route 109 crossing. It was a small place, and everyone was very nice. I must be gaining notoriety in small towns along the Buckeye Trail. The waitress/cook asked me if I was "that guy" in the *Defiance Crescent News*. She encouraged me to write a book about my journey. Maybe I will.

I am camping on the Wenig Family farm in Haskins. I found them listed on my Buckeye Trail map as a camping spot for hikers. Bill and

Camping in the back of a garage at Wenig Family Farm, Haskins

Julie are very nice. They let me camp in one of their buildings where I will be warmer and out of the wind.

It has been a long day. The overcast skies, the cold, and the wind mixed with snow and rain made for miserable hiking conditions. Call it my German heritage determination to lay down 27 miles in this god-awful weather. All I want to do now is sleep.

March 31: Day 12
Pemberville, College Days, and a Missed Opportunity

I hiked 21 miles to Pemberville.

I don't have many nice things to say about the hiking today. It's still cold and windy—unseasonably cold, and it was all road walking except for a quarter of a mile of gravel path. It was a memorable day, though.

Yesterday I said goodbye to the Miami & Erie Canal which I had been following off and on since Dayton. I've now turned the first of Ohio's four corners. As I crossed to the east side of I-75, I was able to get a nostalgic look at the Bowling Green State University campus, my alma mater. College was the best and most fun four years of my life, and I even managed to get a degree! I spent many miles reminiscing about my days at BGSU and what a life-shaping experience it was.

When I went to BGSU as an 18-year-old freshman, I had no idea what I wanted to be. A park ranger? A park naturalist? I liked the outdoors so I thought I wanted to be someone who worked at a state park.

Four years later, I graduated with a degree in Management Information Systems, specializing in computers and computer programming. What a contrast to what I thought I wanted to do. Instead of the great outdoors, a fabric-covered, three-walled cubicle became my work space.

I made a good choice, though. With an Information Technology (IT) degree, I rode the wave of plentiful, well-paying jobs of the 1980s. I've worked the past 27 years in the IT field making a great wage and with enough job flexibility to hike and be outside like I always wanted to be.

I consider myself ambitious and forward thinking, but I can't take all of the credit for the decision to major in IT. I had some encouragement. She was an attractive graduate teaching assistant named Patti

Ostrowski. Patti's course was my first in IT, and I was in love. I never missed a class and always sat in the center of the front row. I dropped hints of my infatuation by inserting her initials into computer code that I turned in for homework.

She noticed. I nearly landed a date when, at the end of the semester, she invited me to play tennis with her. Tennis? I couldn't play tennis. I was a 19-year-old sophomore who spent his free time at the pub with his buddies. In a panic over the thought of the total embarrassment I was sure to experience on the tennis court, I declined and made a quick exit out of the classroom. A missed opportunity, I guess. Every once in a while, though, I wonder how things might have turned out if she had invited me for a date over a couple of beers.

When I was ten miles from Pemberville, I called the village office inquiring about camping options. They gave me permission to camp in the city park. I wasn't looking forward to sleeping outside in the wind and cold, but it felt good to have a legal campsite destination ahead of me.

I arrived in Pemberville about 4:00 p.m. As I crossed the street heading toward the city park, I heard a friendly, "Hey, what are you doin'?" That's how I met Jim Fields, the manager of the recently restored Opera House of Pemberville.

Jim happened to be stepping out of the opera house just as I passed by. He invited me in for a tour. I gladly accepted the opportunity to go inside a heated building, drop my pack, and get off of my sore feet. It had been a cold, miserable day on the trail.

I wasn't sitting for long when Jim said, "Ok, let's do the tour!"

"Is it a walking tour?" I asked. I had been walking all day and was pretty tired. I was hoping that Jim would just tell me about the opera house so I wouldn't have to move.

He laughed at the suggestion of a sit-down tour, "Yeah! Of course it's a walking tour!"

The tour was fascinating. The opera house has been operating since 1892 which makes it one of the oldest functioning opera houses in Ohio. It was once part of miles of land stretching from Lake Erie to Indiana called the Great Black Swamp. Today, Fort Wayne, Lima, and Findlay stand at what once was the southern shores of the swamp.

All we see today is farmland, and we think that's the way it always was. When the glaciers retreated, however, they left a huge swampy area. The swamp was heavily forested, making it so bleak and dark even

The historic Pemberville Opera House, Pemberville

during the day that it was called the Great Black Swamp. The marshy land was thick with mud and travel was slow going for anything on wheels. Malaria was rampant.

The discovery of oil and gas in the swamp drew settlers and prosperity. A town sprang up about every ten miles. Because ten miles was a long distance to travel through the thick, marshy swamp, each town built its own opera house. The one in Pemberville still functions. At 119 years old, the opera house in Pemberville is a valuable relic of Ohio history.

As I thanked Jim for the tour, our conversation turned to my camping plans. Jim suggested I camp in the stables of the American Legion just down the street. The stables are empty, clean, and dry and would provide cover from the wind. He made a telephone call to secure the necessary permission and walked me over there.

I felt so welcomed! The guys invited me to join them and offered to buy me a beer. I declined, but was deeply gratified by their kindness to me. My tent fit fine in a hallway of the stables. The caretaker at the Legion brought out a small electric heater and extension cord so I could stay warm during the night. As he was leaving, he stopped, turned, and reached for his wallet. "Do you need money for dinner?" he asked kindly.

Did he think I was a drifter? I wondered. "Oh! No, thank you. I'm not homeless; I'm a hiker" I replied. I was thankful, but realized that my fears of being mistaken as a vagabond were being confirmed.

Trail magic is unexpected good fortune or an act of kindness provided by strangers to a hiker. This has been a day of trail magic. Pemberville has been such a friendly town. I never experienced this kind of hospitality from strangers on the Appalachian Trail in all my 7,400 miles on it. Chalk one up for Pemberville and the Buckeye Trail.

BUCKEYE
EST. 1959
TRAIL

CHAPTER 4
Two Worlds Out There

April 1: Day 13
Towns and Cities versus Trees and Forest

I hiked 21 miles to the outskirts of Fremont.

I slept until 8:30 a.m. today. I guess I was tired. It was a good night of sleep except for the occasional CSX train which rumbled through town.

Pemberville continued its trail magic. A traveling salesman picked up my tab at breakfast this morning at the local diner. He was impressed with my journey and wanted to help. I stopped by the post office to mail home a few things I was carrying I did not need. The postmaster was very helpful, too.

The route today was entirely on pavement. The first ten miles to Elmore were on roads. The route was scenic as it generally followed the Portage River.

Traffic was light but there were hills and blind curves which made me nervous from a safety point of view. Drivers aren't used to seeing pedestrians on the road and may be startled. When hiking on roads, I try to alert drivers by wearing an orange safety vest and covering my pack in orange. Even so, I am wary of oncoming traffic and get way off the road when in doubt.

Luckily, the second part of the hike today was on the North Coast Inland Trail (NCIT). The NCIT is an all-purpose trail that, when finished, will connect Pennsylvania to Indiana. The Ohio Bikeways rail-trail system is part of the NCIT. Rail-trail is the name given to unused portions of railroad tracks that are sold to municipalities for conversion to bike and walking paths. Rail-trail conversions are occurring not just in the United States, but all over the world. Old rail routes make excellent paths because they were engineered to be fairly flat and straight; inclines are graded. For the hiker and biker, it's a safer way to travel.

The NCIT went right through the middle of Lindsey, a small town of about 450 people. Lindsey's history dates back to the 1850s. No doubt a village birthed by the railroad before the Civil War when the railroad was fast becoming king.

Every so often along the trail, I see a weathered stone railway mile marker or a "W" (to tell the engineer to blow a warning whistle at a road crossing) which reminds me that I'm walking along the path of travel that served as the fastest form of transportation in the early 1900s. The old markers are also a reminder that, just like the canals, the railroads, too, were displaced by faster and more convenient forms of transportation.

I'm starting to appreciate that the Buckeye Trail traverses towns. Wilderness trails, like the Appalachian Trail, route the hiker out of towns and cities, away from civilization in order to keep the hiker in the natural environment. The Buckeye Trail, on the other hand, is about discovering Ohio.

It routes hikers through areas where they can interact with *people* and *places* and experience *past* and *present* events—what I call the *Four P's.* Hiking the rail to trail offers all four of those P's in big doses.

For the first time on this hike, I pulled out my ear buds and phone out of my pack to listen to music. Since I was hiking on a bike path, and not roads, I could relax a little knowing it would be safe. When Louis Armstrong's song "What a Wonderful World" played, a wave of emotion hit me and tears came to my eyes. The song captured the feeling of the moment for me. I feel grateful for the many people it takes to keep the Buckeye Trail going—the Buckeye Trail Association members, the trail supervisors and maintainers, and the many volunteers who sacrifice their time, money, and energy to put this trail here and keep it here. They may not be big trail users or long-distance hikers themselves, but they're out here doing their part to make a good hiking experience available to everyone.

On the North Coast Inland Trail, Lindsey

I also felt good about what I was doing for me. I was giving my body 20 miles of exercise a day, drinking a gallon or two of water a day, breathing fresh air. I felt a natural, physical happiness. I was also experiencing the mental happiness that comes from doing great things for my body.

Long-distance hikers appreciate the connection that exists between the mind and body. Hiking clears the mind, blows out the cobwebs, and lets thoughts flow freely. The mind doesn't control the body, and the body doesn't control the mind. They work together. When the mind and body are in harmony, it's the best feeling in the world. For a few minutes, my feet did not hurt and my backpack weighed nothing. I was on top of the world.

I arrived in Fremont around dark. I am staying at the Old Orchard Motel for two nights. Tomorrow I am taking a zero. After ten consecutive days of hiking, I need a break.

April 2: Day 14
Continuous Steps

I "zero-ed" in Fremont.

The city center of Fremont seemed awfully quiet for a Saturday. A brief rain storm moved in this afternoon, leaving a beautiful rainbow behind.

The Old Orchard Motel is a delightful "mom & pop" place. The motel pre-dates the interstate system and is located on old US-20. The rooms are clean, cozy, and inexpensive. The proprietor did a load of laundry for me at no charge.

The proprietor also dropped me off at the library downtown this morning to use the computer. I caught up on e-mails, blog entries, and uploaded pictures. One of the advantages of hiking the Buckeye Trail (as opposed to a wilderness trail) is that I can stay easily connected. My blog, especially, is having an impact. Friends and family are reading it because they enjoy being "arm-chair" participants in my adventures. I realized the day I met Sam back in Delphos that others are reading it, too. They're people who know about and/or are affiliated with the Buckeye Trail. That's exciting for me. My blog has created a way for me to become an active member of the Buckeye Trail community. It's also created a way for the Buckeye Trail community to get to know and support me.

My plan for tomorrow is to take a taxi to a place about 25 trail miles away, walk back to the motel on the Buckeye Trail, and spend another night here. There are no campsites for the next 70 miles.

The next 100 or so miles are all road walking except for a few miles in Findley State Park. The word is that by this time next year, the Buckeye Trail will be relocated off this long road walk and moved on the North Coast Inland Trail (NCIT) bikeway. For now, this road walk is the official route.

I'm not looking forward to the road walk. However, I consider myself a purist. A purist returns to the exact same spot from the previous day so that his or her journey is continuous, what my friends and long-distance hikers Brent and Amy Anslinger term "continuous steps." I easily could have the taxi driver drop me off 25 miles east of here and avoid walking the road. No one would know. Doing that would involve skipping trail.

Not every long-distance hiker is a purist. The Appalachian Trail Conservancy (ATC) awards a special recognition to hikers who hike the entire trail. Each time I've completed the Appalachian Trail, I signed a statement declaring that I made a good faith effort to complete the trail. I'm an ATC recognized three-time 2,000 miler. I'm proud of that accomplishment.

There's no similar recognition on the Buckeye Trail. Nonetheless, I'm making a good faith effort to hike the entire Buckeye Trail. It's an honor system, and I'm committed to it.

This evening, I found myself watching the *Lawrence Welk Show* reruns on TV. My father always watched *The Lawrence Welk Show* on Saturday nights. As a kid, I thought it was the dumbest show ever because it was so boring. I couldn't imagine why anyone would want to spend an entire hour watching people sing. Now it doesn't seem so bad. It brings back good memories of my dad.

It's almost Hiker's Midnight, a trail term that refers to a 9:00 p.m. bedtime. Sunrise comes early on the trail, and if a hiker wants at least eight or more hours of sleep, he should be in bed by nine. Guess I'd better get some sleep.

April 3: Day 15
Foot Pain and the Mother of Presidents

I walked 26 miles from Lowell back to Fremont.
My first near-marathon day.

The taxi dropped me off at 8:30 a.m. about four miles east of SR-19 and SR-101. I completed a "12x12" by noon and then hiked 14 more miles back to the motel.

The morning was beautiful. It was sunny and crisp. Frost covered the farm fields. It soon became cloudy and windy. Showers moved in about noon. I dashed behind a barn to get out of the rain and put my rain gear on. By the time I got geared up for the rain, it had passed.

The hike today was all on roads and sidewalks except for a couple of miles in Wolf Creek Park along the Sandusky River. The soil footpath walking was a welcome relief for my poor feet. It was short-lived. My feet started hurting about two hours into the hike and hurt the rest of the day. This is depressing me.

Long-distance hikers always have pain in their feet. Feet, as the body's foundation, absorb the impact of a hard surface. It's part of the turf, part of the job. At some point on a long-distance hike, feet adapt to what they are going through. They learn to get stronger and adjust. After 259 miles on the Buckeye Trail, though, I was hoping my feet would have adapted by now.

I got my mind off my feet when I crossed over a pretty creek called Beaver Creek. It was formerly called Green Creek because the water is green. Being a caver, I appreciate the geological process that makes this happen. When subsurface limestone bedrock is dissolved by water, cave systems are created, and nearby rivers and lake water turn green. The town of Green Springs is close by. Green Springs is home to the world's largest natural sulfur spring. Beaver Creek originates from the spring.

The route today went through Fremont and past the Rutherford B. Hayes Presidential Center. Hayes, one of the presidents from Ohio and the 19th U.S. President, was not born in Fremont. He practiced law here. The only other state with as many presidents is Virginia. Both states claim William Henry Harrison (ninth President of the U.S.) who was born in Virginia, but lived in Ohio when he was elected president. The long-standing argument between Ohioans and Virginians is which state gets to claim the title "Mother of Presidents."

I am now on map six of the 26 maps which cover the Buckeye Trail. Because the Buckeye Trail is a circular trail, the maps are not assigned numbers, only section names. Sections are identified by a city or town name or other landmark. I'm in the Norwalk section. I decided to number my set of maps from my starting point in Dayton as a way to track my progress. The miles for each section averages about 55. It takes me about two-and-a-half days to complete a section. Only 20 more sections to go!

The Buckeye Trail has an incredible meander factor to it. To give an idea of the meander factor, the taxi ride was 21 miles. The hike back was 26 miles.

There are a couple of reasons. First, the trail designer uses back roads that aren't heavily traveled as often as possible to make the hike safer for the pedestrian.

Second, the Buckeye Trail is about discovering Ohio, so it's routed by a scenic or historic feature or something special. A typical long-distance trail is designed to take the hiker from point A to point B, as close as it can to a straight line, given the considerations of the topography. Trails may have side trails to scenic or historic places, but the main trail is designed to cover distance as the crow flies.

Sinclair gas station, Fremont

The Buckeye Trail is not designed to do that. A hiker may travel five miles, but then end up being only a mile away from where he started five miles ago. That's a meander factor which is sometimes frustrating.

Correction to yesterday's post: There are two campgrounds in this section. I passed two of them today.

April 4: Day 16
A Look of Despair

I hiked six miles before calling it quits, almost making it to Reedtown. My six miles were either respectable or idiotic. I don't know which.

I am in a farmer's barn dodging the wind, rain, and lightning, waiting to be picked up by trail angel Bill "Shoebox" Beier from Norwalk.

I knew the weather today was going to be rainy and cold. The threat of inclement weather wasn't going to deter me. I had to keep moving. Laying down miles always wins over personal comfort for me. Today, though, the weather shut down this hike.

The wind was a sustained 25 miles per hour, coming down hard hitting my face as if someone were throwing rocks at me. The lightning and thunder were overhead, "Crack! Boom! Crack! Boom!" The surroundings offered no shelter and at 5′11″ I stood taller than anything around me. I felt like a golfer on the green in an electrical storm.

I was soaked from head to toe. The last thing I wanted to be was a conductor for a lightning strike, and the rain made it difficult for drivers on this rural, country road to see me.

I spotted a farm house. I ran down the long lane, and knocked on the door. I stood dripping wet and shivering on the front porch. Everything on me was covered up in rain gear except for a small opening for my face—a bearded face.

I had happened to catch the farm owner home for lunch. The front door opened slightly. "My name is Andy. I'm a Buckeye Trail hiker. I'm caught out here in the rain. Is there any place I could go to get inside?"

She looked at me through the crack. I looked like a drifter. But she saw the look of despair on my face. She saw the look of a stranger who needed help. Somehow she trusted me.

"You can go into the barn," she said through the crack.

"Go into the barn" was all I needed to hear. I ran into the barn and took my pack off. Thankfully, I was out of the wind and rain. But I was still shivering and needed to get dry clothes on and warm up. Shivering is the beginning stage of hypothermia.

I was relieved when Shoebox answered my call. Shoebox is a trail angel. We have never met, but he's a backpacker and found my blog online. He e-mailed me a few days ago to say that he's been reading my blog and wanted me to know that he lived in the area, and did I need anything? Shoebox picked me up within the hour. Shoebox and his family hosted me for the night and made me feel right at home. The warm bed and delicious meal were my second instance of trail magic today.

April 5: Day 17
Are You Bicycling?

I hiked 21 miles to Indian Creek Campground.

Shoebox dropped me off at 10:30 a.m. at the farm where I sought refuge just a day earlier. What a difference a day of rest makes—physically, psychologically, and emotionally.

The route today was entirely on country roads. There was not much meandering, and I held a steady due east course. This was good since the brisk 20-mph wind out of the west was at my back all day. The temperature was in the mid 40s, but it felt much colder. I stayed bundled up all day.

Part of the route today was on Old Military Road. Old Military Road was used during the War of 1812 to move troops and supplies between Wooster and Fremont. This former Wyandot Indian territory was opened for settlement in 1817. The Ohio Historical Society erected a nice plaque in a glacial boulder along the route.

It snowed in Havana today. How do I know? I was there at lunchtime. Havana is so tiny that the only commercial establishment is a tavern. It has no sign. Who needs a sign when everybody in town knows where the tavern is? I would have passed it up if someone had not pointed it out to me. Strangers in the tavern stand out in a small town, especially ones carrying a backpack and poles.

The waitress was curious. "Are you bicycling?"

"No. I'm a hiker."

"Where did you come from?"

"I walked here from Dayton."

"Today?"

"No, not today. I started March 20."

She seemed satisfied with my answers, but the conversation struck me as entertaining. Maybe she didn't know that the sixth largest city in Ohio is 150 miles away by car or maybe she didn't realize that the average foot speed of a hiker is only about 3.5 miles per hour. Nonetheless, the interchange was friendly and after a light lunch, I was soon on my way.

The long road walking started to wear on me today. Miles 17–21 were not fun. A farm dog ran out on the road, barked, and acted mean to me. I acted equally mean back to him and scared him off.

The last mile along US-250 was brutal and dangerous: lots of semis, a narrow shoulder, and a steep ditch. My only consolation today was knowing that soon the Buckeye Trail would have a new, off-road route in this section.

Good news: My new cushioned insoles for my shoes I bought at Dick's yesterday are working. The new insoles are alleviating some of my foot pain from the road walking.

April 6: Day 18
Smarter Than the Average Bear

I walked 19 miles to Findley State Park. So far, I have hiked a little over 300 miles on this journey.

I spent the night at Indian Creek Campground in a rustic camper cabin. The campground is small and compact. The camper cabin looks like a large playhouse for a child. I had to duck to get in. It is lightly furnished with a chair, a bed with a mattress, a small table, and electrical outlets. The cost of the cabin was $20 and for just $5 more, the proprietor included a portable electric heater. The $5 was money well spent.

I stayed in the camper cabin until almost 1:00 p.m. listening to rain and blowing wind outside. I was in no hurry to leave my warm and dry accommodations. I enjoyed two cups of Starbucks instant coffee and a package of chicken noodle soup.

The rain and wind let up, so I hit the trail. I hiked due east all day. The route today was 18 miles on roads and one mile in the woods.

I was able to complete the Norwalk section and started the Medina section of the Buckeye Trail. The Norwalk section was 59 miles of all

Cabin at Indian Creek Campground, New London

road walking. I am getting tired of walking all day on roads, and am glad to be done with it.

Completing a section is a huge psychological boost for me. I read somewhere that the secret to achieving a big goal is to reward yourself by completing a series of small ones. Completing one section is do-able, completing 26 sections is daunting. Finishing the Norwalk section motivates me to finish the Medina section. I am now on map seven, 19 more maps to go.

Because I got a late start to my hike today, I didn't arrive at Findley State Park campground until 7:00 p.m. I'm camping here for the night. I was tired, hungry, and almost out of water. I needed water to heat for dinner and to wash up. But the water faucets in the campground were still off for the winter, and the campground was empty.

I spotted a couple finishing up a hike. I needed water, but it's bad hiker etiquette to directly ask a stranger for a favor. So, I did a "yogi"—but not in the same way as Hanna-Barbera's Yogi Bear and his picnic basket snatching antics in Jellystone. I implied my request with a question, with the same result.

"Do you know where I can get water?" I asked. Being indirect allows the stranger to decide whether or not to offer help. They sensed my disappointment when they told me the nearest operating water faucet was two miles away. I gladly accepted their offer of a ride to the water and back. It was a successful "yogi" and very much appreciated.

April 7: Day 19
I Never Leave Home without Them

I hiked 22 miles to the Lester Rail Trailhead parking lot. All of the miles but one was on roads.

Findley State Park was still deserted this morning. A park maintenance worker drove through the parking lot. He either didn't see me or didn't care that I camped under the picnic shelter.

The road walking and new padded insoles are taking a toll on my feet. I developed several new blisters. None are bad or too painful and are probably the result of changing my shoe insole configuration. I'm discouraged because I've gotten far more blisters on this hike than I did on my 500-mile hike on the Appalachian Trail last summer.

I used my trekking poles today for the first time in several days. I've had them strapped to my pack since the trail was all road walking and the pavement doesn't give like a soft surface. By using them today, they'll change my cadence enough to alleviate some foot pain. I use poles for other reasons, too. Swinging poles gives my arms something to do and engages my upper body in continuous movement, helping to distribute body and pack weight. Poles help me keep a rhythm to my stride. They also come in handy when I need to move a snake off the path or keep mean dogs at bay.

Non-hikers occasionally tease me about going skiing, and when I don't need them, they can be a bother to carry. Using poles properly also takes some getting used to. I've noticed the hikers who run for exercise tend not to use poles. They say they don't need them because they already have strong upper body balance. What they don't realize is that poles offer not only balance, but also stability, reducing knee stress, especially on steep inclines where energy can be transferred into forward momentum. On a descent, poles reduce the impact of upper body compression weight on the knees, feet and ankles. I never hike soft trails without them. It felt good to use my poles again.

The area I hiked through today had lots of ponds. I was surprised by the number of homes that had small ponds. I passed by dozens of them. I heard that 7,800 enclosed bodies of water, including the state's largest natural lake, Chippewa Lake, are in this county. Medina has more ponds and lakes than anywhere else in Ohio and is hoping to be named the "Pond Capital of Ohio." The soil composition has a lot of clay which holds water well. Some of the ponds looked inviting enough for a swim, but most had "no trespassing" signs.

I also noticed a number of oil wells dotting the landscape. A lot of gas and oil is trapped in the shale around this part of Ohio. The first oil well was drilled in Ohio in 1860. Some of the oil pumps looked rusty and abandoned. Others looked new and shiny. None of them were pumping oil.

I am starting to see a change in the topography. There are now gentle hills and slopes instead of wide open, flat land. This makes for more interesting hiking, but also makes the road walking more dangerous. The drivers of cars coming over these hills can't see me until they are upon me. Drivers are reluctant to move over into the other lane when approaching me when they can't see over the hills. That's understandable, but dangerous for me.

A road construction worker warned me to be wary of traffic when school lets out. He said the teenage drivers on the road like to drive fast on their way home. He's right. It seems the youngest drivers are the least likely to move over for a pedestrian. If I get whacked by a car, it will likely be driven by a young, female driver talking on a cell phone.

April 8: Day 20
Pay It Forward

I spent today at the home of a fraternity brother and little sister in Berea.

I have been out hiking on the Buckeye Trail for 20 days. The weather has made this hike miserable some days. On most days, the sun has not been out. The steady wind, the below-normal cold temperatures, and the rainy spring made quitting or at least taking more zero days a huge temptation. I'm sticking with it, though, but certainly not for fame or fortune. Maybe it's because of my German tenacity. Maybe it's the thrill of a challenge. What I think it is, though, is that I'm starting to love the Buckeye Trail and the people I'm meeting on the way.

I am taking a zero day today. When a hiker says, "I need a zero day," there's always a good reason. It could be fatigue—the kind that even a good night's sleep and a good meal won't fix.

Another reason could be to shower, do laundry, or run errands to the pharmacy or the grocery store or the hardware store for stove fuel, or the bank and the ATM.

Today, though, I have three different reasons to take a zero. The weather is cool and rainy; my feet have blisters, and I was invited to spend two nights with Tom and Sharon Farmer. The comfortable, warm bed last night was wonderful. A second night is too good to pass up.

I went to college with Tom and Sharon at Bowling Green State University. Tom is a Delta Upsilon fraternity brother from Bowling Green State University. Sharon was a member of our Little Sister program.

When I was a freshman, I debated whether or not to join a fraternity. The older brothers said the benefits of joining a fraternity extended beyond the college years. They sure were right. At the time, I thought joining a fraternity was about drinking beer and meeting girls. Of course, we did our fair share of that, but the real benefits were the skills I gained as an officer and a service project and charity event organizer. As an 18 year old, I was learning to pay it forward by giving my time and talents for the benefit of other people. Making others' lives better in some way has stuck with me as a life goal. I also formed friendships at Delta Upsilon that have lasted decades. It's good seeing Tom and Sharon again.

April 9: Day 21
An Openness about Them

I hiked 23 miles to Hinckley Reservation.

I felt refreshed and strong from my zero day. The first three miles today were on the Lester Rail Trail. The next 15 miles of the Buckeye Trail were on roads routed around Medina. The last four miles were on trails in the woods of Hinckley Reservation.

The Lester Rail Trail was the first railroad corridor in Medina County to be converted to a hike/bike path. Much to my surprise it has a crushed gravel surface and not asphalt. Walking on the softer surface made for a delightful three miles which went by too fast.

On the path, I met two walkers. There was an openness about them, and we introduced ourselves right away. Mick, Bonnie, and I chatted a bit about my hike and before we parted Mick wanted to do something nice for me. He pulled out four pieces of chocolate from his pocket. They were delicious. It wasn't much, but I was deeply gratified. There seems to be a special connection between traveler and stranger that leads to acts of kindness. We had an instant social bond that I appreciate, but just can't explain.

The temperature hit the mid 50s today, a bit of sun and a slight breeze. The warmer weather brought northern Ohioans out of hibernation. Not seeing other people on the trail is lonely. Not today, though. I saw a lady on a horse, a guy in a kayak, rock climbers, joggers, bicyclists, and walkers—all of us travelers, enjoying the first signs of spring.

The steep, scenic climb up the Whipps Ledges Loop Trail was tougher than I expected. It was more of a work out than usual. I am definitely in rolling terrain.

Whipps Ledges, Hinckley Reservation

Just above Whipps Ledges, I hit the highest point on the Buckeye Trail according to the map. It's a little anti-climactic because it's not an impressive peak with a beautiful vista, like Clingmans Dome in North Carolina or Mt. Washington in New Hampshire. It's a flat field at 1,290 feet above sea level. It may not seem high, but it is higher than some points on the Appalachian Trail.

It was a good feeling to cross to the east of I-71 today. I'm getting closer to Cleveland.

Finding shelter is still my primary challenge on this hike. I am camping on the back porch of a building owned by the Cleveland Hiking Club, an organization established in 1919 to promote hiking. It's one of the oldest hiking clubs in Ohio. The building is still closed for winter, but all I need today is a place to set up my tent. My thanks to Liz McQuaid, a BTA board member, who got me the necessary permission to camp here. Friends of Liz, Jim Fleet and Renie Wirkus, dropped me off at my campsite. Tomorrow, they will take me back to the trail.

I have just seen my first mosquito of the year. Be careful what you wish for. I have been wishing for spring, and it came today. So have the bugs.

BUCKEYE
EST. 1959
TRAIL

CHAPTER 5

The Good, The Bad, The Reality

April 10: Day 22
Good News, Bad News

I hiked 23 miles. It was an exhausting day, and my toughest day on the Buckeye Trail yet. Nevertheless, it was filled with milestones and trail magic.

Milestone 1. Good news: after the first ten miles, I reached a standard double blue blaze, signaling a southbound turn. I'm going south; bad news is I still have northbound miles to go. In the round numbers, the last 180 miles that began near Toledo and ended near Akron have been on all roads except for about 20 miles. For me, it means the end of the "Great Road Walk," as I have not-so-fondly dubbed it. Good news: the next 60 miles will be almost entirely off roads—trails in the woods and canal tow path. My sore feet will be happy to be off of pavement.

Milestone 2. Good news: I'm at the end of the Medina section and am starting the Little Loop. The Little Loop is a north-south circular trail off the main circuit, a.k.a., the Big Loop. It's a five-section loop over 200 miles long comprised of an East and West branch. The end of the Medina section brought me to the intersection of Akron and Bedford on the loop. From here, I can head either north on the Buckeye Trail to Lake Erie or south to Akron. I decided to hike south to Akron. Once I get to the bottom of the Little Loop, I will flip-flop back to the intersection where I started and hike north to Lake Erie. Bad news: it's a good plan, but I have yet to figure out the logistics.

Milestone 3. Good news: I have completed one-quarter of the Buckeye Trail in both days and miles. "Woot, woot!" for reaching milestones. Bad news: milestones are just intermediary goals in the big scheme of things. So, maybe just one "woot."

As I discovered today, being "off road" did not mean I was on "easy street." A change from the moderate temperatures of the last few days caught me by surprise. By midafternoon, the temperature soared to around 80 degrees. I hiked in shorts and a tee shirt for the first time.

The last ten miles were in the woods of Cuyahoga Valley National Park. It's the only national park in Ohio. It's a very beautiful area and despite its proximity to urban areas, has a surprisingly remote feel.

The trail, though, was very strenuous for me. The map says the Buckeye Trail undulates gently in this section. I say it goes straight up and down. No switchbacks, no grades. When the trail wasn't steep, it was muddy, the shiny kind of mud that's rain soaked and slippery and makes for hard going.

I was exhausted by the heat, the mud, and the hills. Faucets in the park were still off for the winter. I was thirsty and running short on water. I needed to find a water source.

I'm always careful when choosing drinking water. Rivers have a lot of environmental contaminants as do streams around farm areas; ponds and lakes aren't ideal sources either, especially ones colored with algae. Plus, I don't want to repeat an experience I had on the AT in 1998. I had picked up a parasite from my water supply. I was on the 100 Mile Wilderness Trail in Maine when I got slammed with symptoms of giardiasis—gas, bloating, cramps, diarrhea, and weakness. It lasted two weeks and made for miserable hiking.

Luckily, I happened across a small, flowing creek. It was my best option for water. But to my shock and dismay, I discovered that I only had enough Aqua Mira drops to treat a half liter of creek water. It wasn't much, but enough water to keep me going.

By late afternoon, I was sunburned, parched, and starting to worry about dehydration. Some unexpected and much appreciated trail magic came my way at Blue Hen Falls when a couple with small children, without asking, handed me three bottles of water. How did these trail angels know I badly needed water?

I was grateful and pressed ahead. By 8:30 p.m., I made it to the Stanford House, a youth hostel that allows camping, located on an

Trail in Cuyahoga National Park

historic 19th century farm. I was hot and thirsty again, and the hostel was closed for the season. Then, much to my surprise, three hikers came out of the woods and gave me a quart of Gatorade, a soda pop, and two protein bars. I could finally rehydrate. Then, I found a gallon of water that my cousin John Spitzer and his fiancée Erica (who live in the area) had stashed for me. They also left a root beer. I drank three liters of liquids in no time. I wonder if these hot temperatures are here to stay. I'll be better prepared next time.

I set up my tent in the chicken coop turned wood shed. It was dark, dingy, but dry. I ate supper and went straight to bed. I am one tired camper, but what a day! Life is good on the Buckeye Trail.

April 11: Day 23
A Last-Minute Rendezvous

I hiked nine miles to the Hunt Farm Visitor's Center.

I awoke to rain this morning. I was glad I set up camp in the chicken coop. I stayed dry. The roof leaked only a little bit. By 11:00 a.m., I was on trail and hiking in a light rain. Today, I'm hiking entirely in the Cuyahoga Valley National Park, a sprawling 20,000-acre national park between Cleveland and Akron. This river valley has been a scenic venue for recreational activities since the 1870s.

The trail from Boston to Peninsula was entirely in the woods. It was a little less undulating than yesterday and a very pretty walk. Daffodils were blooming where the former homes of the first Western Reserve settlers once stood.

From Peninsula, the Buckeye Trail follows the Ohio & Erie Canal Towpath Trail, the major trail through the national park. Several years ago, the National Park Service converted the towpath into a multi-use trail that follows the Ohio & Erie Canal. The towpath trail is flat, wide, dry, scenic, and rich with history. I passed the remains of Lock 27 Johnnycake Lock, Lock 28 Deep Lock, Lock 29 Peninsula Mill Lock today. Johnnycake Lock got its name in 1828 when several canal boats ran aground in heavy silt caused by a spring flood. The stranded passengers and crew ate cornmeal bread called Johnnycakes until they could be rescued. Lock 28 Deep Lock's special feature is that it's deep. At 17′, it's a foot deeper than Lock 8 of the Miami & Erie Canal. Lock 29 Peninsula Mill Lock, built as an aqueduct over the Cuyahoga River, is a reminder what an impressive feat of engineering and architecture the Ohio canal system was.

I ended my hike today after only nine miles at Cuyahoga Valley National Park's Hunt Farm Visitors Center in order to spend some time with my sister, Cindy. I don't see her often. Cindy lives and works in Detroit. She is driving from Detroit on the Ohio Turnpike for a business meeting in Pittsburgh tomorrow. Our paths happened to cross today when she realized from reading my blog that I was near the turnpike. We made plans to rendezvous for a cup of Starbucks coffee.

Cindy is two years older than I am, the oldest of five, and the only girl in the family. She was the model firstborn—confident, competitive, driven, and responsible. When I was struggling to maintain B's in school, Cindy was the straight "A" student. While my piano playing skills were so-so, Cindy excelled. In fact, she excelled in everything she did. Growing up, I never thought of Cindy as the nurturing, motherly older sister. She was the eyes and ears of Mom and Dad. If we four boys were into mischief or had a secret, it was best not to let it slip to Cindy. She reported all suspect activity with neutrino-like speed.

While I did my best to avoid Cindy's watchful eye as a kid, as an adult, I admire her. Her drive and ambition provided the blueprint of success for me and my brothers. Her Harvard MBA landed her high-powered executive positions and board room seats in corporations where her ideas are valued and respected. I learned from watching her how successful kids who grow up in middle class families can be. I learned that applying oneself leads to success. I realize and appreciate the positive impact she has had on my life.

We were glad to see each other today. We chatted about my hike, about work, about family; we had a good visit. She dropped me off at the home of my cousin, John Spitzer, in Stow. I will spend the night with John and Erica. It felt good to be with family today.

I am looking forward to the rest of the Akron section. There are more good things to come.

April 12: Day 24
Springtime Blues

I hiked 24 miles to Barberton,
at the southwest border of Akron.

John dropped me off at Hunt Farm at 7:45 a.m. The weather was cloudy and breezy, with temperatures in the mid 40s. The sun never came out today. A few rain drops fell. Two days ago, the temperature was in the 80s. I am discouraged by today's gloomy, cold weather.

The Buckeye Trail followed the Ohio & Erie Canal Towpath Trail today except for jaunts into O'Neil Woods and Sand Run, both managed by Summit Metro Parks. The tow path trail was care-free hiking: level, wide, and dry. Leaving the tow path trail to hike in these two parks was not a welcomed change for me. The jaunt took me a short distance on busy roads and up a steep hill. Plus, O'Neil Woods has not allowed the Buckeye Trail Association to paint the familiar blue blazes that are so important to help guide the Buckeye Trail hiker. No blazes require more focused attention on path conditions and closer map navigation.

O'Neil Woods, Summit Metro Parks

The Buckeye Trail goes through downtown Akron because the Ohio & Erie Canal goes right through Akron, dividing east Akron from west Akron. The city of Akron doesn't permit blazing either. It was quite a task to follow the tow path trail through a large city. I relied on the section map for directions and descriptions.

After leaving the industrial area of Akron, the trail follows the canal through an economically depressed area. For almost 100 years, Akron was the "rubber capital of the world" because it was corporate home to several big name tire manufacturers. Economic forces drove the last rubber company out of Akron over 20 years ago.

It was a bit strange hiking through a blighted area. But I fit in well. I say that because I still can't shake the out-of-place feeling I get walking through urban areas wearing a backpack. Maybe it's just the gloominess of day that's making me feel down.

I felt even more down when I saw flowering Skunk Cabbage in the parks. Skunk Cabbage, named for its bad smell, is a low-growing wild flower that can make an appearance as early as February. It's an amazing plant that can grow and bloom in cold temperatures because it generates its own heat. Amazing or not, it's April. Skunk Cabbage was growing in Dayton a month ago. Spring should be well underway. I knew spring came later in northeast Ohio, but I didn't realize by a whole month. I feel like I'm stuck in a time warp.

April 13: Day 25
I Get by with a Little Help from Family and Friends

I hiked 15 miles to Crystal Springs, the southern junction of the Little Loop. This means I have completed the Akron section, Map 8.

The sunshine and clear skies washed away the spring blues from yesterday. The temperatures reached the mid 50s, and the skies were mostly sunny. Quite a change from yesterday. I gave John and Erica bear hugs goodbye. They were wonderful hosts. I hope to make it back for their wedding in October.

The hike along the Ohio & Erie Canal Towpath Trail was a very beautiful section with a surprisingly remote feel. For many miles, the path was a narrow strip of land between two bodies of water—the canal on one side and the Tuscarawas River on the other. It felt like I was hiking on a linear island.

Lots of people were enjoying the trail today—walkers, joggers, cyclists. I waved to all of them. Most waved back. Waving is an ancient form of communication demonstrating that you have no weapon. Even today an open hand shows peaceful intent. Today, I was happy and friendly.

For the first time since the Great Road Walk, I listened to music on my smartphone. When the U2 song "Beautiful Day" played, I belted out the lyrics as loudly as I could: "It's a beautiful day . . . Don't let it get away . . . It's a beautiful day." I have no special vocal talent, but the joy of the moment was too overwhelming to hold inside.

I saw many painted turtles sunning themselves on logs in the canal. I saw a small garter snake on the trail soaking up the sun. He lay motionless and let me take several photos of him. There was nothing special about this little guy, and I've seen 100 garter snakes in my lifetime that look just like him. But today he seemed to be enjoying the trail as much as I was. We were sharing a happy moment together.

In Crystal Springs, I was met by Paul "Used To Could" Lynch from Mayfield. Paul is hosting me for the night. I met Paul last year on the Appalachian Trail in New Hampshire.

Our friendship started like some friendships start on the trail—by lending a helping hand. The day we met, I happened to spot Used To Could heading off in the weeds on a game trail. "Hey, buddy! I'm Captain Blue. I think you missed a turn. The white blaze is this way!" I pointed. He was grateful for the guidance, and we became friends quickly.

We had a lot in common. We were both long-distance hikers; we were both hiking solo; we were both section hikers; we were both from Ohio; and we were both headed toward Katahdin. We were both in the final stretch of an end-to-end hike on the Appalachian Trail—my third complete Appalachian Trail hike and Used To Could's first. We hiked together off and on for five weeks.

I happened to be ahead of Used To Could on the trail when I reached Monson, Maine. Monson is a destination spot for hikers doing the 100 Mile Wilderness Trail. Anyone starting or finishing the 100 Mile Wilderness Trail has to pass through Monson. Monson is also known for its black slate mines. John F. Kennedy's grave stone was quarried here, and the sidewalks are made of black slate that become very slippery when wet.

I was in Monson on a rainy day to re-supply before tackling the rough terrain of the next 100 miles when I slipped and fell on slick, slate sidewalk. I jabbed my big toe. The next day, my purple and swollen big toe hurt like heck. I was concerned and debated what to do. The 100 Mile Wilderness Trail is not a leisurely stroll in the woods. Cell reception is poor and help would be slow in coming if I needed to get off trail. Parts of the trail are treacherous and an injury, even a small one, can be a death sentence under certain conditions.

Just about then, I ran into Used To Could. It was a lucky meeting. He listened to my toe tale and within the minute, put me on the phone to a medical doctor—his son. I described my symptoms and my concerns. Much to my relief, the doc didn't think it was broken. I was back in business! The next day, I hiked with Used To Could and Gail, his friend from Ohio, who was joining him on this section of the trail for a while. It wasn't long before I jumped ahead, and we parted ways.

I ran into Used To Could one last time on the Appalachian Trail a few weeks later—at the top of Katahdin, the northern terminus. We finished the 2,179 mile hike the same day. What a happy coincidence! About three million people attempt the Appalachian Trail every year. Only about 15,000 have ever finished. I'm proud to say that Used To Could and I are among them.

Paul and I drove back to his house where Laura, his wife, had prepared a delicious dinner. Gail and her husband also joined us. We reminisced and talked trail. What a special bond we have! What a wonderful reunion! Life is good. It was a great day to be a hiker or a reptile.

April 14: Day 26
Flip-Flop to a Northbound Hike

I hiked 20 miles to the Harper Ridge Picnic area in the Bedford section. It will take me to Lake Erie. I am looking forward to seeing Lake Erie, turning south, and finishing the Little Loop.

I began the hike at the northern junction of the Little Loop of the Buckeye Trail where the Medina, Akron, and Bedford sections meet and hiked south. That was four days ago. Now I'll be turning around and hiking north.

Paul "Used To Could" Lynch hiked with me for a few miles today. We didn't hit the trail until 11:00 a.m.

Today's hike was in the "Emerald Necklace." A bird would say that the circular shape of the Cleveland Metroparks parks looks like a green band. It's a system of 16 preserves and reservations (including the Cleveland Zoo) and eight golf courses, many of which are linked. Together, they form a nearly complete circle around the Cleveland metro area. The Emerald Necklace is 21,000+ acres and hundreds of miles of hiking, biking, and horse trails.

The route today was mostly in the woods on a soil footpath, a pleasant surprise and a pretty walk. Hemlocks line the trail starting at Bridal Veil Falls. At first look, the falls do not seem that impressive, but the water from the falls starts a 100′ descent over shale rock into Tinker's Creek Gorge. It's a sight that rivals the most scenic parts of the Appalachian Trail.

Bridal Veil Falls, Cleveland Metroparks

I finished the hike around 7:15 p.m. Paul and I had stashed a car at the Harper Ridge Picnic Area earlier in the day. I drove back to Paul's house for the night.

April 15: Day 27
The Trail Becomes Your Home, and the Journey Becomes Your Life

I hiked 17.5 miles to the Chagrin River just past North Chagrin Reservation. I hoped to hike a little farther but it was a good spot to stop.

The weather was nice today! The temperature was almost 60°, and it was sunny. Paul "Used To Could" hiked with me for the first hour.

Shortly after Paul turned back, I saw two young ladies ahead of me on the trail. I don't have a special gal back home, and it's hard to meet girls on the trail. So, I put my boots in high gear, caught up with them, said "hello," and walked right by. At the next turn, I got out my map and purposely acted a bit confused about where I was. By then, the two ladies caught up with me . . . which was my plan.

"Hi, I'm Andy. I'm hiking the Buckeye Trail. Do you happen to know how far it is to Chagrin Falls?" I asked. Yep, it was a pretty lame pick-up line, but it worked. Their names are Ginni and Dawn. We chatted for a few minutes, and I took their photo. I gave them one of my business cards and thanked them for not being afraid of me. Dawn replied that she is from Newark, New Jersey, and it takes a lot to make her afraid. Either I'm not as scary looking as I thought or big, burly, bearded guys are a common sight in New Jersey. We exchanged farewells, and I was off, happy for the brief moment of female companionship.

I took a coffee break at Look About Lodge, an 80-year old log cabin constructed from chestnut trees. I unpacked my alcohol stove to make a cup of Starbucks instant coffee and study the map. I realized this very spot is 999 more trail miles to Deeds Point where I started. The remaining miles are now less than a thousand. Woot!

The route continued on the Emerald Necklace along the Chagrin River, a state scenic river. Soon I came to the end of the woods walking. For the next seven miles, I walked along Chagrin River Road, bordered by large estates and farms on one side and the Chagrin River on the other. I stayed alert for traffic since it was Friday afternoon and traffic was picking up.

Just before reaching North Chagrin Reservation, I saw a car slow down and heard a voice shout, "Hello, Andy!" It was Gail "Gimley" with whom I had dinner two nights before. She drove out to hike with me. When we reached North Chagrin Reservation, we met Used To Could. The three of us hiked together for a few miles. It was great to have company. We finished the North Chagrin Reservation, the point where the Buckeye Trail diverges from Cleveland Metroparks, and I decided to call it quits for the day. I am spending my third and last night with Paul and Laura Lynch. They are wonderful hosts.

Paul and I have a special friendship. It's common on the Appalachian Trail to strike up lasting friendships. The trail becomes your home, and the journey becomes your life. Fellow hikers you connect with become your family—you watch out for each other, you trust each other, and you share common experiences. You know what it's like going without a hot meal, a hot shower, and a soft bed for days at a time. You're accepting of body odor, dirty fingernails, and an unshaven, unkempt appearance. In these ways, Used To Could is part of my hiker family, and I'll always value our friendship.

April 16: Day 28
A "Buckeye Trail Hiker" Hat

Today and tomorrow will be zero days for me. No hiking. The windy, rainy weather make them good days for a zero.

My next host, Debbie Zampini, picked me up from Paul's house today. It was a "host-to-host Andy hand off." Debbie lives in Chardon, in the middle of the Little Loop. She has generously offered to shuttle and host me until I finish the 150 miles or so I have remaining of the Little Loop. Debbie is the vice president of the Buckeye Trail Association; she's also on the board of trustees, and is the section supervisor for the Bedford section where I'm hiking now.

Debbie took me to the Sport Rack shop in Chardon. I am having a hat made with the words "Buckeye Trail Hiker" embroidered on the front and "Buckeye Trail" on the back. I plan to wear it while I hike. People who see me will know what I am doing even if they don't speak to me. I want people to trust me. In my experience on the Appalachian Trail, hikers are generally trusted by the locals. I've been picked up for rides or offered accommodations by good-hearted strangers many times. It's a little different with this urban, suburban, rural hike I'm on. A hiker in full gear walking down a road, on a bike path, or in a neighborhood arouses suspicion. I hope the hat will make people curious and not fearful. The hat should be finished Tuesday.

Debbie invited me to accompany her to the Cleveland Zoo for EarthFest 2011 tomorrow. Cleveland's Earth Day celebration is the longest-running, largest environmental education event in the nation and attracts 50,000 people every year. Debbie will be volunteering at the Buckeye Trail Association (BTA) booth.

Eastern box turtle

April 17: Day 29
I Met a Girl Named Maria at EarthFest

I am taking another zero day in Chardon.

The day started with some bad news. Debbie's pet cat had a stroke last night. We awoke to find Good Girl paralyzed in her rear legs. Debbie rushed Good Girl to the animal hospital but returned home alone. She had to put Good Girl down. Debbie was visibly shaken. Good Girl was the first pet that she had ever lost. I felt very bad for her. She later told me that she was happy that she had my broad chest and sympathetic shoulder to cry on that day.

Despite her loss, Debbie wanted to stick with our plans for the day. She thought going to EarthFest would help to take her mind off Good Girl. By the time we arrived at noon, there were several thousand people at the zoo. It was buzzing with activity. There was live music, local and organic food, and over 170 exhibits promoting care for the environment, eco-friendly life styles, health, and fitness.

I could sense that Debbie wanted to be alone, so I offered to work her shift at the booth. It helped her grieve just to be able to roam the zoo.

The weather was cold that day, but there was a constant flow of visitors to the Buckeye Trail Association booth. The Cleveland Zoo is in the city. EarthFest attracts a lot of people from the urban Cleveland area and the Buckeye Trail Association booth is often their very first introduction to long-distance hiking. A lot of people I talked to today didn't know that long-distance trails exist and that people actually hike long distances on a trail.

Even though I had only been on the trail three weeks, I was feeling happy about my accomplishment. Plus, I had a good story to tell. "Hi, my name is Andy," I said, "and I walked here from Dayton." It was a really powerful opening line that got people interested. Their first reaction was, "No way!" And my response was, "Yes, I did, and it wasn't in a straight line either. I walked it via Toledo!" So there were a lot of questions, a lot of surprised looks, a lot of curiosity, and a lot of disbelief.

One lady did not believe me. I reassured her that I did, but she didn't look convinced. Another lady, Kim, was so intrigued by my journey that she gave me a hug! I have hiked 7,400 miles on the Appalachian Trail, and I don't ever recall getting a hug from someone for being a hiker. One fellow asked me if I needed any money. I answered, "No" but suggested that he could make a donation to the Buckeye Trail Association. He took out his wallet and made a $40 donation on the spot.

I was having a great time talking to people and answering questions when an attractive gal about my age caught my eye. I could tell she was interested in the Buckeye Trail and in my story. She was different from anybody else who had stopped by that day, and my attraction to her was instant. We chatted about hiking and the Buckeye Trail. I gave her a card with my contact information and promised to order section maps of the Little Loop for her. She gave me her address. Her name is Maria.

Debbie and I left just before closing. I never did see any of the animals at the zoo. When we arrived home, one less cat greeted us at the door. I could tell that Debbie was grieving the loss of Good Girl.

I am heading back on the trail tomorrow rain or shine. Looks like it will be rain.

April 18: Day 30
You Must be Captain Blue!

I hiked almost 20 miles into Mentor.

Maria sure has a pretty name. I googled her e-mail address last night to tell her so and to say that using her first and last name, I found 13,625 anagrams. I've seen a thousand sunrises on the trail. The sun never rises on the horizon in the exact place twice. Sometimes, a man has to take a chance. She must have been impressed by my creative pick-up line because we have a date tonight. I need to be in Mentor by 6:00 p.m.

I resumed hiking today where I left off two days prior—North Chagrin Reservation. Not good hiking weather today. The temperature was in the upper 30s and rainy, but I have happy thoughts of Maria to keep my mind off the crummy weather.

The road walking was scenic. A fellow retrieving his garbage can at the end of his driveway walked down the road with me a bit to chat. It was nice to have his company.

As I made my way to Chapin Forest, the rain got harder, and it was taking a toll on my body temperature. I was wet and cold.

Chapin Forest is known for its ancient rock formations of sand and pebble which created ledges of parallel rock layers of differing widths. It also has a lodge for cross-country skiing. The lodge was closed for the season, but there was activity inside. I knocked on the door to ask for water, hoping I could get inside to warm up. The employee who answered turned me away. As I stood on the porch dripping with rain water, I asked again. He indicated that the nearby restroom was unlocked. I made myself at home on a bench in the men's room across from the urinal and ate lunch. At least it was warm and dry. It appears once again that I was mistaken for a homeless person.

After lunch, I headed back out in the rain. From an overlook in Chapin Forest, I could see the shoreline of Lake Erie, 18 miles away. I'll reach the northern terminus tomorrow! Woot! I am ready to reach Lake Erie and make the turn to the south.

Seeing Lake Erie put a spring in my step and I was soon in Penitentiary Glen. It is known for the 130′ gorge that divides the park.

Because the walls of the glen are steep, people say it got its name because it is easy to get into but hard to get out of, like a prison. One legend says that Civil War prisoners were held there.

I stopped inside the Nature Center at Penitentiary Glen. It's located in a beautifully restored barn that was once a part of an early 20th century family farm. The Glen now belongs to Lake Metroparks.

When I arrived at the Nature Center, the Lake Metroparks employees, much to my surprise, greeted me with, "You must be Captain Blue!" Debbie had phoned ahead to tell them about me. The receptionist got me a cup of hot coffee, chocolate, and peanuts. The naturalists at the center gave me a personal tour. I learned a lot about the glen and its history. Here they treated me like a celebrity long-distance hiker. What a contrast to my experience at the ski lodge!

I was wet and cold, but I made it to Mentor on time. Maria was there waiting. I smiled when I saw her. We enjoyed a delightful dinner in Willoughby and good conversation. She drove me back to Debbie's place at the end of the evening. We made plans to see each other again.

April 19: Day 31
"I'm Going to Hiawassee"

I hiked 18 miles, reached the northern terminus of the Buckeye Trail and ended in Painesville.

It is a cold, windy, rainy, overall miserable day. But it felt good to be hiking. It gave me the chance to think about my date with Maria last night. We have a lot in common. She was raised Catholic like me. She's in the IT field like I am. She loves the outdoors, to camp and hike and is an adventurous person. I sense that she understands what motivates me to set a goal and then spend three months weathering adverse conditions and hardships to fulfill it.

The winds were blowing hard and the temperature was in the upper 30s when I emerged from the sandy path at Headlands Beach State Park at 2:15 p.m. I have reached Lake Erie and the Northern Terminus. Woot! This is a milestone for me. I have now finished one-third of the Buckeye Trail.

For a hiker, reaching a milestone destination is purely psychological. There's no prize for being partly finished or almost finished.

BUCKEYE
EST. 1959
TRAIL

Lake Erie, Mentor

However, reaching a milestone does serve a purpose. It serves as motivation to keep going. An Appalachian Trail thru-hiker was once asked where he was headed. His response was, "I'm going to Hiawassee," giving the impression that his end point was Hiawassee. Hiawassee is only 70 miles into a 2,179 mile trail. He was actually going to Maine. But in his mind, he was only going 70 miles, and that was a small enough number to digest to make him feel like he was accomplishing something.

I set those types of goals, too. I call them intermediate destinations. They are usually spots with significance—a target destination like Lake Erie. As important as it is to pause to savor the moment when reaching a goal, today's moment was hard to enjoy on such a blustery day. My celebration was a quick picture of the sign marking the northern most point on the Buckeye Trail and an even quicker turn southward.

I was cold, wet, hungry but happy when Debbie picked me up at the southern end of the Greenway Bike Trail in Painesville. I'm glad to be finished with the great trek northward and, on such a wintry-like day, glad that I'm in the warm and welcoming home of a trail angel.

Northern terminus of the Buckeye Trail, Headlands Beach State Park

April 20: Day 32
Things Seem to be Changing

Today I hiked 17 miles to Chardon. It was a busy day.

My hike today took me through Girdled Road Reservation, along Big Creek, and into Big Creek Park in Geauga County. I was on the trail by 8:00 a.m. The weather changed quickly from a balmy 60 degrees to cold, wind, and rain. I needed to find cover for a morning break. Unfortunately, the only cover available was under the SR-608 highway bridge over Big Creek. I climbed down the embankment and found a dry spot under the bridge. Munching on a snack out of the rain and the flying spray of wet cars, I felt like a troll under a bridge.

My route took me to Big Creek Park. When I walked in the front door of the Nature Center, someone asked if I was Captain Blue. I felt like a celebrity for the second time in two days. The folks at Big Creek Nature Center wanted to know more about my hike. I gave a mini interview. They tweeted about my visit and posted a photo of me on their Facebook page.

I was also met there by Patti Cook. Word of my journey is making its way through the Buckeye Trail family grapevine. Patti is the section supervisor for the Burton section where I am currently hiking. She's new to supervising and asked for suggestions about where hikers would find the blazes most helpful in the Burton section. It was nice to meet her.

Continuing on, I was soon in the charming town of Chardon. Chardon was established in 1812 and is the only incorporated town in Geauga County. It lies just 10 miles south of Lake Erie in the Great Lakes Snow Belt. This year, Chardon got 151 inches of snow. That's over 12 feet!

An interesting historical fact about this area is that it was part of the Western Reserve and formerly claimed by the Indians, the French, the English, and after the Revolutionary War, New York, Pennsylvania, Virginia, and Connecticut. Connecticut was the last to relinquish ownership in 1795.

Chardon has a town square and buildings with New England-style architecture. Another interesting fact is that in a few days, Chardon will be hosting the annual Geauga County Maple Festival. At age 82 (this year), it's the oldest maple festival in the United States and one of the largest. I was also surprised to learn that Ohio is in the top 10 states of maple syrup production.

While in town, I met with a newspaper reporter for the *Chardon Maple Leaf*. It's my third newspaper write up about my hike in the last 25 days.

Tonight, Debbie and I will be dinner guests of Gayle and Jim Wohlken, a couple who are strangers to me. They had left a note for me at the Nature Center earlier in the day with their contact information and later called to invite me for dinner. The Wohlkens, who live in Burton, understand what it means to be a long-distance hiker. Their son, Shane "The Gimp" Wohlken, is a Triple Crown Hiker. He hiked the Appalachian Trail, the Pacific Crest Trail, and the Continental Divide Trail and received a lot of help from strangers along the way. They want to help me out if they can. I was surprised, amazed, and gratified when Jim told me that he looked for me on the trail earlier in the day carrying homemade cookies and a pot of hot coffee. No one has ever shown me such kindness on the trail before.

Something is happening on the Buckeye Trail that I didn't expect, and something I never experienced on the Appalachian Trail (AT). The AT belongs exclusively to hikers. There are predictable places to stay, resupply stops every few days, and an abundance of trail angels. Fellow hikers aid and assist whenever needed. There's a code of ethics and of proper conduct. There's a sense of belonging on and off the trail. In short, the AT hiker has the benefit of a well-established, full-fledged community.

In contrast, Buckeye Trail hikers don't experience the support of a long-standing hiking community. I have yet to see another backpacker. There is no detailed guidebook, no signage, no predictable places to sleep and the constant feeling I am out of place has been with me from the start. Neither does the Buckeye Trail belong exclusively to hikers. I share it with cars, bikers, pedestrians, and, at times, skate boarders and roller bladers. Sometimes private property owners share it with me. Now, a month later, things seem to be changing.

The challenges are still unfolding, but the more I'm able to network and build relationships, the more I sense a community growing up around me—a Buckeye Trail hiker community of people who support me—the Wohlkens, Patti, the cordial employees in the Nature Center, the reporter in Chardon, and all of the people who've helped me make it this far. I have spent the last five nights in the home of Debbie Zampini, a kind hearted-person I have known for only a week. The Wohlkens offered to host me tomorrow, and I recently received four other offers from good people who also want to help. I'm feeling cared for and supported, and most of all, special for being a Buckeye Trail hiker.

BUCKEYE
EST. 1959
TRAIL

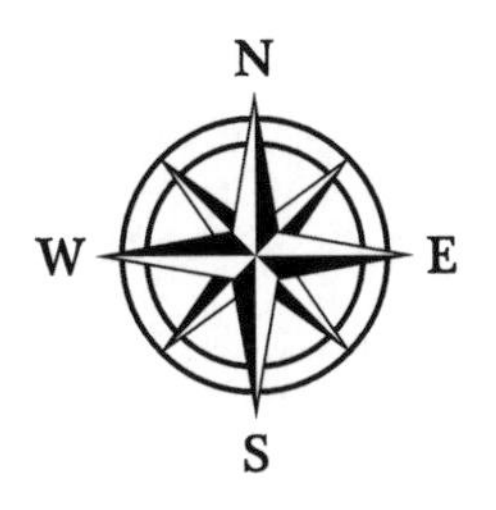

CHAPTER 6
Love Needs a Heart

April 21: Day 33
Present, Past, People, Places: A Big Dose

I hiked 21 miles to Hiram.

I resumed hiking on the Maple Highlands Trail bike path around 8:00 a.m. It's a former Baltimore & Ohio Railroad corridor. From Chardon, the trail runs about eight miles to Headwaters Park. The trail was deserted this morning except for me.

Headwaters Park and much of the land I hiked along today is owned by the city of Akron. The park is so named because it lies very close to the source of the Cuyahoga River. Akron's municipal water supply comes from the Cuyahoga River. Akron owns a lot of land up river in order to protect its watershed from development. The Geauga Park district leases the 926-acre reservation from the city. It's an arrangement with mutual benefit. The park district protects the quality of the water supply for people and aquatic life and also provides opportunities for the public to learn about and enjoy nature.

The 2.5-mile hike through Headwaters Park was scenic and easy. The trail through the woods was wide, dry, and made of crushed gravel. I spotted Skunk Cabbage still in bloom, a reminder that it's still early spring. By the way, there's nothing edible about this "cabbage," at least until it's cooked or dried. The roots of this stinky plant are toxic when eaten raw. Native Americans used it as a medicine.

New section of trail, Burton

I arrived in Burton around 11:30 a.m. and spent an hour with Jim and Gayle Wohlken at their home. They fed me pizza, coffee, and homemade chocolate chip cookies. Jim is very knowledgeable on the history of the area.

After lunch, I met Patti Cook in the town square. We visited the Burton Log Cabin, a working sugar house. It's owned and operated by the Burton Chamber of Commerce. In the spring, the Chamber taps the maple trees, collects sap and produces maple syrup for the annual pancake breakfast. Since 1951, thousands of people have been showing up the first Sunday in March for breakfast. Burton's nickname is "Pancake Town USA."

After sampling the maple treats at the Log Cabin, we hiked a new section of the Buckeye Trail which will open soon. This section is about a mile long and reroutes the hiker from roads and sidewalks to woods and farm fields. Making the Buckeye Trail safer for the hiker is a continuous project.

The rest of the day was a pleasant, 12-mile scenic country road walk into Hiram. Hiram is home to Hiram College. Its most famous alumnus is James A. Garfield, the 20th president of the United States, and one of eight Ohioans to become president.

I'm meeting Maria in Hiram. Maria lives in Cleveland, is single, and has no children. She is a writer, artist, web developer, and a fireball of energy with an unbridled passion for adventure.

I waited for Maria in front of the post office in Hiram holding a blue plastic cup (that I found in the gutter) filled with daffodils (that I picked from the yard of a former homestead along the trail) and a chocolate bunny (that I bought in the local pharmacy). I'm trying to impress her. At the least I want Maria to know that I've been thinking about her all day and am excited to see her.

When she arrived, I could tell by her smile she was pleased with my effort. Tomorrow and the next are zero days. I'm spending them with Maria.

April 22: Day 34
We're Falling in Love

I took Good Friday and Saturday of Easter weekend as zero days.

Maria is from a large, Roman Catholic, Italian family. She is the youngest of eight. Maria lives in Old Brooklyn, a west side neighborhood of Cleveland. Just like the borough of Brooklyn on Long Island, it's an urban mix of ethnicities and cultures—German, Italian, Polish, Ukrainian and Hispanic. Old Brooklyn's original settlers were mainly European farmers who migrated from Connecticut beginning in the 1800s.

My first order of business was to get a haircut. I went to Mario's Barber Shop on Broadview (part of a former Indian Trail) in Old Brooklyn. Mario's is an Italian-owned family business that still offers hot towel shaves and shoe shines. I got both my hair and beard trimmed. Maria got her hair cut down the street.

We stopped in for lunch at the Little Polish diner. It was packed with people who were enjoying the last of the Lenten specials. We had cabbage and noodles and potato cakes.

Maria still owns her collection of old albums and a turn table. We spent the night listening to artists of the late 1970s and early 1980s and reminiscing about college, growing up in big families, and places life had taken us. We love the music of Jackson Browne. The old songs brought back many good memories for both of us. We talked for hours. We're getting to know each other. We're falling in love.

April 23: Day 35
A Woman Driven by Passion

Maria and I awoke to a sunny, 70° Saturday morning.

Maria took me to breakfast at a bakery owned by an Italian and a Ukrainian. There was a line out the door for pastries and breads this morning. So many different ethnic groups are represented here in Old Brooklyn. Each seems to have unique foods for celebrating Easter. At the bakery today, the lamb cake was a big seller. The shape of the cake holds religious significance. In the European Christian tradition, it represents Christ as the "lamb of God."

Maria loves the cultural diversity she finds in her neighborhood. The more time I spend with Maria, the more I'm drawn to her. She's fun; she's creative; she's a woman driven by passion. One of her passions is her dedication to finding solutions to community problems. Maria considers herself something of a community activist.

A few years ago, she moved into a run-down, 90 year-old bungalow that she refurbished as part of an Old Brooklyn neighborhood revitalization program. It's what got her excited about community service projects. She took me to visit one of her completed projects.

On a 60′ wall next to an empty lot in Old Brooklyn is a mural of blue sky, rolling green hills, and countryside. The mural came about because of Maria's efforts. She won a grant award to revitalize storefronts in Cleveland. For this particular storefront (Mr. E's Inn Restaurant), she found the location, the design artist, and organized the preparation, the necessary city approvals, and the volunteers.

The painters were college students, neighbors, and patrons of Mr. E's, and even passersby who were happy to lend a hand. Maria wanted a simple piece of art that would remind the members of the community what Brooklyn Township once looked like during its days as the "Greenhouse capital of the United States."

She wanted the mural to contrast the urban Old Brooklyn of today. It's one of the prides of the community. I understand why. It's beautiful.

Later, we enjoyed a hike at Big Creek Metropark in Cleveland. Maria is an active member of the Friends of Big Creek. It's a group that is trying to acquire and preserve land in the Big Creek watershed. This watershed drains 38-square miles from eight municipalities. The pollutants from these urban areas are threatening the health of the watershed and the aquatic ecosystem it supports. Just like me, Maria loves the outdoors. She cares deeply about issues that threaten nature and is proactive in its preservation.

Tomorrow Maria and I will say goodbye for now. She is spending Easter Sunday with her family, and I need to get back on the Buckeye Trail to resume hiking. I'll miss her.

April 24: Day 36
Dayton Hikers is My Hiking Club

I hiked 20 miles to Ravenna. It's a rainy Easter Sunday.

Maria dropped me off in Hiram around 9:15 a.m. in a steady rain. It rained for most of the day. I was wet and muddy in no time. The first part of my hike was on country roads. Nobody was on the roads except the earthworms and me.

Just before the town of Mantua, I took a lunch break in the rain on a park bench. This is not my first long-distance hike on Easter, but it is the first Easter I've ever eaten lunch sitting outside on a bench alone in the rain eating wet food. I have no family obligations on Easter. I don't have any special traditions or reason to stay at home. Being outside today brought back good memories.

On this day a year ago, seven other backpackers and I woke up to a sunny Easter morning at a Five Rivers MetroPark in Germantown, Ohio. They were newbies to backpacking. I was their guide. The trip was short—an overnight introduction to what it means to carry on your back everything you need to live outside. We hiked in five miles, set up camp, cooked dinner, colored Easter eggs, and had a great time. All were members of Dayton Hikers.

Dayton Hikers is my hiking club. I founded it in 2009. I wanted to create hiking opportunities in the Miami Valley that were free, convenient, and frequent. Ohio has wonderful trails, and my passion is hiking. The timing was right, too. As an IT guy, I saw that electronic social

White pine plantation in Camp Asbury, Hiram

media and the Meetup platform created the perfect venue for getting people out of the house and hiking.

I jumped in with both feet. I created a web page, negotiated discounts on gear for Dayton Hikers members at local hiking stores, started booking a Dayton Hiker's booth at outdoor events, bought banners, printed business cards, scheduled hikes, recruited hike leaders, and planned social events and presentations to give members the opportunity to learn more about hiking. I managed to get the word out that Dayton Hikers was here. In just 18 months, we're at 650+ members, 20 hike leaders, and still growing. It's a good feeling knowing that people back home are out hiking today—rain or shine—because of my efforts.

I finished the rainy 20-mile hike today about 5:00 p.m. The Wohlkens picked me up. I am staying with them tonight at their home in Burton.

I reached a few intermediate goals today. They're not as big as milestones, but still satisfying:

- I crossed over the Ohio Turnpike for the last time.
- I also crossed the Lake Erie-Ohio River continental watershed divide at the Headwaters Trail. Water east of the

divide runs to Lake Erie and the North Atlantic. Water west runs into the Ohio River, the Mississippi River, and empties into the Gulf of Mexico.

- I finished the Burton section at the end of Camp Asbury and entered the Mogadore section. I'm now on map 11, 15 more to go.

"How do you catch a cloud and pin it down?"

April 25: Day 37
The Picture Captured a Great Moment

I hiked 22 miles almost to the Mogadore Reservoir.
It was a warm, wet, and rainy hike.

The Wohlkens loaded me up with homemade chocolate chip cookies and a box of chocolates made in Burton. They dropped me off near the Ravenna Arsenal around 11:00 a.m.

The Buckeye Trail follows the perimeter of the Ravenna Arsenal for several miles. The Ravenna Arsenal, owned by the United States Military, was used during World War II to produce munitions and ordnance. During World War II, it spread across 21,000 acres, included 1,300 buildings, and employed 14,000 Ohioans. It manufactured more munitions during the war than any other plant in the United States. It is still a large facility. Jim Wohlken told me that Ravenna was selected as a munitions site because of the high number of annual overcast days. Clouds made it harder for the enemy to take aerial photos.

It has now rained for two straight days. The trail through West Branch (of the Mahoning River) State Park was woods walking. It was saturated with rain and exceptionally muddy. There's a term hikers use for this kind of mud—*boot-sucking*. The mud is so deep that your whole boot disappears into the mud and when you pull your foot out to take a step, sometimes the boot stays behind in the mud, literally sucking it off. It makes hiking difficult, and today it slowed me down.

The highlight of my day was fording a flooded section of the Buckeye Trail. The trail went down into a ravine to the lake in West Branch State Park. The water was so high that the trail was completely submerged. My options were to backtrack, bushwhack to higher ground, or to go

Flooded trail, West Branch State Park

through the water. The two options didn't seem like a good use of my time and energy. So, I chose the most direct route, the water.

I plunged into the water and sank in the mud. The water was knee deep in some places and thigh high in others. What fun! It was a photo opportunity I couldn't pass up. I spotted an old tire floating down stream. I pulled it close, carefully positioned my camera on the bobbing tire, set the timer, and waded to mid-stream to pose. It was a great shot.

The picture also captured a great moment. A few weeks ago, I was feeling discouraged by the weather and mud. A few weeks ago, I would not have chosen to wade up to my thighs in muddy, cold water. But I'm tougher than I was a few weeks ago, mentally and physically, and more confident that I can do what it takes to continue. Now I'm enjoying the challenge. I've reached a new phase of the hike.

There's a heartiness, a certain mental and physical stamina, which comes from being on the trail. It evolves as a hike unfolds. You can be fit, logistically prepared, and geared up, but on the trail, you're in an environment that's unpredictable. Nature is unpredictable. There is no plan for every circumstance nor can you anticipate everything that will happen. That's when the hike becomes a mental game. Your adrenaline kicks in. You become more resourceful at confronting obstacles.

Challenges are expected. Problem solving gets easier. It's part of the resilience of trail rhythm that develops on long-distance hikes.

So it was no big deal when, a mile later, I again had to ford the swollen stream. (Note to mother: I would not have attempted these crossings in swift-moving water.)

To add to the challenges of the day, a hard rain hit on the way to Mogadore Reservoir. I was soaked all over again. The last three miles were tough hiking—lots of mud, slick areas, downed trees and limbs from the recent storms. The trail was an obstacle course. I fell once when I bent down to maneuver my way under a tree. I landed softly in a mud puddle. No bruises or scrapes, just mud.

Close to 8:00 p.m., the rain let up. So I called it quits for the day and made camp. I found a dry campsite perched on a gravel mound above the reservoir.

The beavers swimming below slammed their tails on the water and made a loud splash to alert other beavers that I was there. It was a fine place to end a wet day of hiking.

"How do you keep a wave upon the sand?"

April 26: Day 38
Today was One of Those Days

I hiked 17 miles and ended near Hartville.

It was a pleasant morning. No rain last night or this morning. I enjoyed a cup of coffee along the shore of the Mogadore Reservoir and watched the sun rise.

My route took me through the Mogadore Reservoir and past the hangar for the Goodyear blimp. Goodyear has a large facility near Mogadore for its airship operations. All three blimps must be traveling; I didn't see any today.

The pleasant day turned hot, humid, and windy. I was walking into a 15–20 mph wind. I'm not a small guy by most standards. At 5′11″, 220 lbs., I can manage a moderate wind. But this headwind blew me from side to side. It wore me out. I took a break in the front yard of a farm house. I plopped down in the shade of large tree, took my shoes off and lay down. The owner of the house gave me a friendly wave while he cut the grass. I recovered quickly and was back on the road.

Goodyear Blimp hangar, Mogadore

Being a pedestrian all the time has its occasional disadvantages. Today was one of those days, especially for a man in love. My plan is to hike until this evening, then hitchhike to a hotel in Hartville. Good plan? Bad plan? Hitchhiking is a form of travel that became popular during the Great Depression. Unlike other states, it's actually legal in Ohio. I've done it many times in many states and have met some interesting people along the way. But the logistics can be tricky. Getting a hitch when you need it to the place you need to be can be unpredictable, and Hartville isn't exactly a destination point in this rural area unless you're Maria and me. She's coming to spend the evening with me there.

It was on my mind when, on Griggy Road, a car stopped ahead of me and two people got out. They walked towards me. I didn't know what to think. So far on this journey, I've had good encounters with strangers I've met. I've not been harassed as a homeless person, stopped by law enforcement as suspicious, or threatened from property owners for trespassing. But they waved and asked if I was Captain Blue. It was Dana Zintek and Lisa Daiber. They are members of the Buckeye Trail Association. Dana is the section supervisor for the Akron section. Lisa is the newsletter editor. They have been following my journey online and came to help.

It was actually a moment of trail magic. They gave me water (which I sorely needed since I was still drinking lake water from Mogadore Reservoir), chocolates, and offered to transport my pack so that I could hike at a faster pace. At the end of my hike, Dana and Lisa took me to lunch at a nice restaurant. Then they dropped me off at the hotel in Hartville where I was planning to spend the night. I enjoyed their company and conversation and was appreciative that I didn't have to hitchhike. It was a bit of trail magic and like all trail magic, came when I least expected it and when I needed it most.

"How do you hold a moonbeam in your hand?"

April 27: Day 39
What It Means to be a Hiker

I hiked 21 miles, just past Crystal Springs north of Massillon. I've now hiked over 600 miles.

The morning was very windy with an ominous-looking sky. Dark clouds loomed on the horizon. Rain drops spit from the sky. The weather report said to expect winds of 20–30 mph. I felt every bit of it. The gusts of wind were blowing me around on the road.

It brought flashbacks of traversing a treacherous mountain peak called Mt. Madison in the Presidential Range of the White Mountain National Forest in New Hampshire in 2003. That day in the Whites, I was alone and hiking above tree line at about 5,000′. This particular summit, as with the series of summits I was to make through the Whites, is strenuous and often dangerous because of the wind. Storm winds blow in from the coast and blast their way through the range, sometimes reaching speeds of over 200 mph. The cold wind can drop body temperature to lethal levels of hypothermia in a matter of minutes. This was my third Appalachian Trail hike, and I was well aware that many hikers had perished in these mountains.

As I made my way up, the trees that had been protecting me from the wind disappeared into nothing but rocks and moss-covered boulders, scrubby, wind-blown spruce, and low-growing bushes and plants. It was cold and windy. I layered up with every piece of clothing in my pack—hats, gloves, sweaters. Anything that wasn't tucked in or tightened down flapped violently. My hood was pulled tightly around my face, but the wind cut through the opening, smacked my face, and pounded my ears. The noise was deafening, like the roar of jet engines. I was leaning into the wind with full force trying to make headway. The clouds above were zipping from ridge to ridge as if in fast forward. I felt afraid. I retreated back to the safety of the tree line.

I set up my tent and hunkered down, hoping the weather would change. I waited for two hours. But if I didn't leave soon, the chances of getting off this ridge before dark would vanish. I gathered the courage to try again.

I reached the ridge and battled the wind using my poles and strong legs as points of contact. Then it hit. A gust of wind blew me off balance and literally picked me up off the ground and into the air. Amazingly, I landed gently on my feet. It was like the hand of God had reached down, picked me up, then set me on the ground. I had never in my life felt so helpless in the face of Mother Nature.

Today on the Buckeye Trail was a small reminder of what it means to be a hiker—constantly exposed to the elements. I was thankful for the rest in Green and refueled with a hearty lunch. Around 6:00 p.m., I arrived in Crystal Springs—another intermediate goal met. Crystal Springs closes the Little Loop. Two weeks and 251 miles later, I'm now back on the main circuit of the Buckeye Trail.

I paused, looked back north, and reflected on what a wonderful experience the Little Loop had been. Some wonder what purpose the Little Loop serves besides adding miles to an already long trail. For me, it bolstered my confidence that I can master this trail. I saw sights I had never seen before; I found my trail rhythm and discovered a supportive Buckeye Trail community that I didn't know existed; and I met Maria. Smiling to myself, I turned south.

I met Maria tonight at Riffil's Riverside Tavern in Massillon, between the Tuscarawas River and the Ohio & Erie Canal. Maria is here with her camping gear. We camped in a back lot of the tavern along the river. The patrons of the Tavern are quite interested in our story. A guy from Dayton goes hiking through the area and meets a girl from Cleveland. She joins him along the trail and shares his company. Matt, a patron, wanted to do something nice. So he drove home, got a bottle of wine, and brought it back for us. That was very sweet of him.

Shelf mushrooms along Ohio & Erie Canal towpath trail

April 28: Day 40
Life Is Better on the Buckeye Trail

I hiked 18 miles to Bolivar. The route today is almost entirely on the Ohio & Erie Canal Towpath Trail except for the last mile into Bolivar.

Maria and I ate breakfast at Riffil's Tavern. Matt, who had given us the bottle of wine the night before, was there and picked up our breakfast tab. I guess Emerson was right, "All the world loves a lover." Maria and I hugged goodbye. She hopped into her car, heading north for work, and I headed south on the Buckeye Trail.

The dark morning clouds gave way to blue skies, sun, and puffy clouds. It was a bit windy but otherwise a fine day for hiking. I have finally reached spring! The grass is green; the trees are leafing out, and plants are growing. I saw trillium in bloom for the first time. I stopped by the post office in Massillon to mail winter gear home. A streak of cold weather is still possible; I may need these items, but I am anxious to lighten my load.

Today begins a new phase of the hike. I am now out of range for weekday visits from Maria. It is time to focus on getting to the halfway point. The terrain also changes. The transition from glaciated Allegheny Plateaus to unglaciated means more hills to climb. The nature of the trail changes, too—fewer cities and places to stay. Nevertheless, I've set my sails to the wind, so to speak. Time to lay down some miles.

In the town of Navarre, I stopped in the local coffee shop for a break. It was ladies' card-playing day. When I walked in the front door, 14 sets of female eyes looked up from their cards and stared at me. It was a "spaghetti Western" moment, and I was Clint Eastwood. Card playing and chatter halted. All eyes turned to the stranger who walked through the door. This stranger was dressed, not like a cowboy, but a hiker, who had a beard and carried a backpack.

"Hi, I'm Andy. I'm hiking the Buckeye Trail!" I said in the friendliest voice I could muster.

The ice broke and for the next few minutes, I was flooded with questions—which I answered to the best of my ability. Once their curiosity was satisfied, card playing and chatter resumed. During a light lunch, a shirt on display caught my eye: "Life is Better in Navarre." To me, life is better on the Buckeye Trail. What a great shirt that would make!

My destination for the day was Bolivar. Before reaching town, I tried to find a place to camp in or near town. I called the village office and got no answer. I called the canoe livery and got no answer. I called the local police department, but the fellow on duty was a part-timer and not from the area. I called the sheriff's office. They came up empty handed. The guy at the bike/hike shop in town said to just sneak into Fort Laurens State Memorial and camp there. There's a term hikers use in this instance. It's called stealth camping or camping undetected in a place where camping is not allowed. It's risky, but necessary when there's no place else to go. I've done it many times and was prepared to do it tonight.

Then I remembered that a fraternity brother, John Boron, lives in North Canton. John served as fraternity president, and I served as vice president during our senior year. Juli, his wife, was the president of our Little Sister program. I shot off an e-mail to John. He offered to pick me up for the night. Their dog, Ginger, is a sock thief. One of my socks is missing. Ginger won't tell where it is.

"How do you find a word that means Maria?"

April 29: Day 41
Enough Risks for One Day

I hiked 19 miles to New Cumberland. Not too bad for getting a late start at 1:00 p.m.

The hike today was filled with history. Just past Bolivar on the Ohio & Erie Towpath Trail, the Buckeye Trail goes through the location of the former Fort Laurens. Fort Laurens, built in 1778, is the site of the only battle of the Revolutionary War that took place in Ohio. The British led a party of Indians in various attacks against the fort in 1779. The remains of the 20 soldiers buried here were excavated in 1973. In 2003, as part of Ohio's Bicentennial, one set of remains was placed in a special tomb and was dedicated as Ohio's Tomb of the Unknown Patriot of the American Revolution. Over 8,000 Revolutionary War heroes lived in Ohio.

The trail continued on the canal towpath to near the historic town of Zoar. Zoar was founded by German immigrants who fled Germany to escape religious persecution. The settlers lived a communal lifestyle for almost 80 years in the 1800s. Today, Zoar Village is an Ohio historic site.

The Buckeye Trail picks up the North Country Trail on the east just past Zoar and exits west at Napoleon. At 4,600 miles, the North Country Trail is the longest of the National Scenic Trails and traverses seven states from New York to North Dakota. It's one of the nation's eleven national scenic trails with the same congressional designation as the better known Appalachian Trail and the Pacific Crest Trail. The North Country Trail and the Buckeye Trail share about 800 miles of trail in Ohio.

The day was uneventful until I received an e-mail from Mary Hamilton, the Massillon section supervisor. She wrote that the Tuscarawas River had flooded parts of the trail and advised an alternate route. Just a few weeks before, flooding was so bad along the Tuscarawas near Zoar that roads and schools were closed. Floods this year have been record breaking.

My first reaction to being told I can't do something risky is to do it anyway, or at least try. I pressed on. Mary was right about the flooding. The trail looked like a lake but the water was moving too fast and

Ohio & Erie Canal towpath trail, Bolivar

too deep. I decided it was not wise to attempt to navigate it. But the detour would cost premium miles. I spotted a railroad bridge over the Tuscarawas River.

I scrambled up the muddy embankment to get to the level of the tracks and surveyed the risk of walking the bridge. The span over the water appeared to be about 200' in length with 100' feet of ramp at either end, and an additional portion suspended above SR-212. The bridge had a deck of open grating with a six-inch or more gap between each tie. There was no foot path, no side walls, no hand rails over the water, and no place to go except 50' down into the water below.

It was no time for vertigo or acrophobia. The only other option I allowed myself was to cross a flooded trail. In my mind, walking the tracks was a safer choice (or at least a drier choice). I carefully stepped from tie to tie, hoping I wouldn't be numbered among the 500 pedestrians killed by a train each year. I arrived safely on the other side, and scrambled down to SR-212, hiking the road until I passed the flooded area and overall, feeling lucky that doing something so dumb worked out OK.

Around 6:00 p.m., I took a short break to check phone messages. Mary offered to host me for the night. She knew there were no camping sites in the area. My plan had been to hike until dark and sneak into the woods to stealth camp. Mary's offer was better. I had taken enough risks for one day. She picked me up around 7:30 p.m. and took me to her house in Dover.

In addition to being a section supervisor, Mary is a trail maintainer and caretaker for the Buckeye Trail Association Barn near Tappan Lake. I like Mary's ideas on trail maintenance. At times, she gets help with maintenance from people who are sentenced to perform community service for minor crimes they commit. Picking up trash in the woods or clearing trail isn't as easy as other types of community service and offenders who get a taste of the hard work of trail maintenance don't always return for a second day. It is, though, a novel way to help keep the trail maintained.

"How Do You Solve a Problem like Maria?"

April 30: Day 42
Without a Master Plan

I hiked 18 miles to Tappan Reservoir along US-250.

Mary dropped me at the trail about 11:00 a.m. It's perfect hiking weather. The sun made an occasional appearance from behind the clouds and temperatures were in the low 60s.

The route today was mostly on windy, hilly rural roads except for two stretches near Leesville Lake and Tappan Reservoir. The topography of the land has definitely changed. I am out of northeast Ohio. Gone are the straight, flat roads. In their place are rolling hills and windy roads. Hiking is more difficult now with lots of ups and downs. It's much more scenic, too.

Hiking along Leesville Lake, part of the Muskingum Watershed Conservancy, was especially beautiful. For a man-made lake, it rivals in beauty to the natural glacial lakes region of the AT in Maine—pristine blue bodies of water that fill the valleys between the mountains—or in this case, the hills.

The Buckeye Trail goes through the small town of Bowerston, population 398. As I was walking through town, five young boys playing basketball spotted me. One yelled to me and asked if I was a hiker. I yelled back that I was, and I had walked over 600 miles. That piece of information was all it took. The boys immediately stopped the game, and with basketballs in tow, ran up the hill to check me out. They were

Young boys, Bowerston

curious, and seemed a little awe-struck. They wanted to know about hiking and living on the trail—where I sleep and what I eat. I gave each one my card. When I asked for directions to the convenience store, the littlest one piped right up. He wanted to make sure I knew to turn right at the white car. He was spot on. Who needs an address, map, or coordinates when you have a six-year-old giving you directions?

Mary picked me up at the Tappan Dam area at 5:45 p.m. and gave me a ride to the Buckeye Trail Association Barn on Tappan Lake. The Barn, over 100 years old, is a field house for BTA events. Many volunteers have donated their time, material, and money to renovate it. In its former days, the barn stored grain, farm equipment, and housed livestock. Since leasing the barn a few years ago, the Buckeye Trail Association added a kitchen, dorm rooms, bathrooms, showers, and an open meeting area as part of its renovation. It's dry, but unheated. Mary left a heater and curtains so that I could enclose a small area in the dormitory. It was warm and dry.

There is not a shelter on the whole Appalachian Trail that is this nice! Maria arrived soon after with a crock pot dinner for us to enjoy. She's spending the evening with me.

How Do You Solve a Problem like Maria? from *The Sound of Music* has been playing in my head for the past several days. The similarities between Maria in the movie and my Maria are there—rambunctious, free-spirited, determined, loving.

And just like the movie, there are all kinds of things to figure out about Maria. I live in Dayton. Maria lives in Cleveland. How do we have a relationship when we're 300 miles apart? Ours didn't start out as a traditional romance. We weren't two people looking for love. We were both busy doing other things when we met.

Falling in love was not part of the plan for this journey. Love is a journey of its own. It just kind of happens without a master plan. It leads you down a path to an uncertain destination, unfolding day-by-day.

How do I court her properly? Will her friends and family think I'm a drifter? How do I gain their respect? How do I keep my mind on the trail when my heart wants to be with this incredible woman? How do I solve a problem like Maria?

BUCKEYE
TRAIL
EST. 1959

CHAPTER 7
Rain, Rain, Rain

May 1: Day 43
The Fountain of Youth is on the Buckeye Trail

Today ended up being a zero-mile day. No hiking. The morning brought gray skies and a steady rain.

I had originally planned to hike today with Ray Ferrell, a trail maintainer for the Bowerston section. But with the rain and the cold, it was a good day to stay indoors, and also an opportunity to spend another day with Maria.

Maria and I left the Barn only once today when we went out to eat at the Express Cafe on Tappan Lake. When our order arrived, the waitress brought a large plate of food for me, "I hope you are hungry!" She smiled as she set down the plate.

"No problem!" I smiled back.

All long-distance hikers are familiar with the term "hiker's appetite." It's a ravenous appetite that kicks in after a few days on the trail. Hiking puts a great physical demand on the body. The energy required for constant, strenuous movement typically requires at least twice the caloric intake. A normal diet of 2,000-3,000 calories per day translates into 4,000–6,000 on the trail.

On a long-distance wilderness hike, it's difficult to consume the necessary calories. Fresh food has a short trail life, and it's inconvenient to carry because water content makes it heavy. So, hikers worry if they will have enough food to make it to the next resupply or the next town.

On the AT, eating establishments sometimes cater to "hiker's hunger" by offering challenge meals. There's a hiker hostel in Monson, Maine that offers patrons a pin-on button if they can finish the largest serving on the menu—a huge breakfast of pancakes, eggs, toast, and sausage. With Monson the last town before the 100-mile wilderness, many northbound AT hikers (a.k.a. "nobos") take on the challenge like it's their last meal.

When we were done eating, not a single dinner roll or pack of crackers was left on the table. I had eaten everything!

Maria left in the afternoon. For the rest of the day, I enjoyed the solitude of the barn. It was beautiful by the lake. There wasn't much to do, but this was fine with me since my goal on zero days is to rest and relax. By late afternoon, the rain had stopped and the temperatures rose to the mid 60s.

I'm hoping May will be drier than April was. It was the wettest April ever on record in Ohio.

Two weeks from today, I celebrate a milestone birthday—one of those birthdays when your age ends in a zero. I have always remarked that hiking on the Appalachian Trail is my personal fountain of youth. Long-distance hiking makes me feel young and strong. I am delighted to discover that the fountain of youth is on the Buckeye Trail too.

May 2: Day 44
A Treasure of Ohio History

I hiked 21 miles, just past Clendening Lake.

I hiked another part of Ohio that I've never seen before, and had a guided tour to boot. Ray Ferrell, a trail maintainer in the Piedmont Lake area shuttled me to my starting point and then met up with me ten miles later so that we could hike together. We were expecting to hike all day in the rain. Luckily, it rained only in the morning before we started.

Ray is my trail angel today. I always welcome the opportunity to hike with trail maintainers or section supervisors. I enjoy their company. They're the ones familiar with the conditions of the trail and the location of the blazes. It also gives me a better appreciation for the difficulty of the work that they do especially in remote, wooded sections. Only lovers of the Buckeye Trail think hauling chain saws, axes, and

High water, Tappan Lake

other tools for miles over rough terrain and then doing back-breaking work all day is fun.

Ray and I hiked the Clendening Lake region together. Clendening Lake is the largest non-commercialized lake in Ohio and is part of the Muskingum Watershed Conservancy District. It's hilly. It's strenuous, but beautiful. The trail in Harrison County is the prettiest part of the Buckeye Trail I have seen. The region has gently rolling hills and several lakes. The area is wooded and the trail feels remote in many places. I didn't realize this beauty existed in Ohio.

The effect of the wet and windy spring is evident. The woods are a lush green now. Spring wild flowers are blooming everywhere including the trail. The wind has littered the trail with limbs and branches. Blowdowns make wonderful habitats for all kinds of creatures, but are a nuisance when they cover the trail. We moved fallen limbs as we hiked. Ray noted the large fallen trees we saw covering the trail so that he and his crew of volunteers can clear them. Keeping the Buckeye Trail open for hikers is a never-ending task.

After the hike, we ate dinner at a cafe in Freeport. Freeport is one of the smallest towns on the Buckeye Trail. It has a total area of .60 square miles and a population of 369. Its post office has been operating since 1814. It seems every small town I've been in was founded in the 1800s. It amazes me that these small towns have endured war, economic downturn, and social and cultural upheaval. Pat Spain, the local librarian, is a wealth of information about this area. She joined us after dinner at Ray's invitation. The library is the hub of activity in this small town, and a local hiking group has just formed. We talked about the Buckeye Trail and posed for a few photos for the library Facebook page.

Afterward, Ray gave me a tour of the Freeport Lockup. I relish discovering these treasures of Ohio history. The Freeport Lockup is a small, one-room jail cell made from sandstone blocks. It was in use from 1895–1937. It's cold, damp, and sparsely furnished. The only view of the outside is through a small, open-air barred window. This late 19th-century mini-dungeon is not a place you'd ever want to be locked up in. I wonder if hikers mistaken as vagrants were obliged to spend the night here.

I'm so glad I have a warm, dry place to sleep tonight. It will be my third night at the Barn. Ray will shuttle me to Clendening Lake in the morning so I can resume my hike. I appreciate his support and company on this journey.

May 3: Day 45
"Yeah, right"

I hiked 15 miles to Hoop Road near the line between Harrison and Guernsey County.

It rained most of the day. The temperature never rose out of the 40s. It was a cold and miserable rain. The route was on back roads except for a five-mile stretch of woods along Piedmont Lake. The roads are lightly traveled, windy, and very scenic. At times, the road feels like a wilderness trail—quiet, peaceful, with minimal human contact.

I left the Clendening Lake region and entered the Piedmont Lake region, another Muskingum Watershed Conservancy District project.

On the way, I passed by the Lake Piedmont Inn and took a break from the rain on the front porch. The inn is closed for repairs until the fall. But I made myself at home on the large covered porch anyway and heated up a cup of hot coffee. I called the owner to let him know I was here. He was very friendly. I like to alert local residents of my presence so I won't arouse suspicion and possibly end up in the modern version of the Freeport Lockup.

Several miles later, I wandered into the campground of the Piedmont Lake Marina looking for a place to escape the rain. I was wet and muddy. The men's restroom was open. So, I plopped down on the floor and took a break. If I had had the time, I would've hiked over to the main building of the Marina. A legendary 50 inch, 55-pound muskie, caught in Piedmont Lake in 1972, is on display. Seasoned anglers have been coming to this lake ever since in hopes of breaking the 39-year muskie state record.

It has rained 16 out of the last 30 days. I'm getting tired of hiking in the rain. The first 15 days of this journey were in cold and wind. These last 30 days have been wind, rain, heat, and cold. There's a saying on the trail that there's no such thing as bad weather, only bad gear. My response to that is, "yeah, right."

When I arrived at Hoop Road, I called Jim Spain. Pat Spain, whom I met the day before, and Jim live about a mile from the Buckeye Trail. I gladly accepted their invitation to spend the night if only to get out of the rain. I've had so many instances of trail magic on this journey. Jim and Pat are trail angels number 20.

The Spains own 230 acres with lots of woods and a pond. I took a hot shower and did a load of laundry. Jim cooked the morel mushrooms he had collected a day earlier. This is the first time I had eaten morel mushrooms. They were delicious! I can see why people hike the woods to collect them. These spongy-looking mushrooms are a gourmet's delight. They have a gourmet price tag, too, and can fetch up to $30 a pound at the market.

May 4: Day 46
The Halfway Point

I hiked 20 miles, just past Salt Fork State Park. I'm halfway!

I enjoyed a hearty homemade breakfast with Pat and Jim. We drank coffee that he roasts and donates to his church to sell as a fund raiser. He gave me a bag. His brand name is Journey Java. It seems appropriate to be enjoying Journey Java on my milestone day.

The weather today was characteristic of the last 45 days of this hike—windy, rainy, cool. The many little ups and downs on the trail today reminded me that I was in the rolling hills of southeastern Ohio. The route today was all on back roads except for about four miles of trail walking in Salt Fork Wildlife Area. The back roads were deserted. I hiked for almost four hours before a car passed me.

I walked by the Jim Morrison cow pasture. I swore the mooing of the cow sounded just like Jim Morrison of the Doors and a few lines from "L.A. Woman." What a talented cow! It's a hard song to moo. Maybe the solitude of the trail today is playing mind games on me.

At 5:00 p.m. today, I calculated that I reached the halfway point on my Buckeye Trail hike.

On a circular trail, the halfway point is dependent on the starting point. There's no definitive point, no marker, no signage like there is on a linear trail to let hikers know how far they've come and how many miles are left to go. Buckeye Trail hikers have to add up section miles completed and section miles left to go to calculate the mid-point, which I did.

When I arrived at that point, I pulled out a pen and two sheets of notebook paper from my pack, and in block letters, made the following sign: "DAYTON via Old Man's Cave and Cincinnati, 722 miles" with an arrow pointing toward Dayton on the first sheet. I placed the second sheet beside it and wrote: "DAYTON via Akron and Defiance, 722 miles" with an arrow pointing the opposite direction. I laid both sheets on the ground on a patch of dandelions. Between the two sheets, I positioned a Buckeye Trail tri-fold brochure with the words: "The Buckeye Trail, Linking the Four Corners of Ohio" on the cover.

The brochure was a nice touch, I thought, given the spontaneity of the idea to record the moment with a hand-made sign. Just as I was about to snap the picture, it started to rain. I let out a big sigh, got a shot of my wet tribute, and hurriedly stuffed it back into my pack.

Halfway points are bittersweet for me. I put so much time and energy to get here that I am happy to be half finished but, then again, after all this effort, I have the equivalent to go. I am only half way done.

I have no personal traditions to celebrate midpoints. But a well-known hiker tradition when nearing the halfway point of the 2,179 mile Appalachian Trail is to partake in the half-gallon challenge. Pine Grove Furnace General Store (in Pine Grove Furnace State Park in Pennsylvania) offers a commemorative spoon to any hiker who can

Halfway point, Salt Fork State Park

down a half gallon of Hershey's ice cream in one sitting. It's a memorable way for the hiker to celebrate and a great way for a little camp store to sell a lot of ice cream. In principle, the goal is to eat robustly.

When a turkey hunter I met at the Barn Yard Campground where I was spending the night offered to drive me to a convenience store, I decided to celebrate and eat robustly. I ordered ten pieces of fried chicken and a six pack of adult beverages to celebrate passing the halfway point. I ate eight pieces of chicken and drank five beverages. Wilbur and Orville, here I come!

May 5: Day 47
Excitement of Historic Proportions

I hiked 21 miles to Seneca Lake, the southernmost lake of the Muskingum Watershed Conservancy District's lakes.

The route today was on curvy back roads except for about five miles of hilly woods walking near Seneca Lake. Like Clendening and Piedmont, Seneca Lake is another beautiful, man-made lake. It's the largest of the ten permanent Muskingum Watershed Conservancy District's lakes.

It's also notable because it's located in Noble County, the youngest of Ohio's 88 counties.

I took a side trip into the town of Old Washington to mail a few items home. The post office was closed until 12:30 p.m., so I had some time to look around. Old Washington, population 279, was settled in the early 1800s. Three Confederate soldiers are buried there. They were members of Morgan's Raiders, a unit of Confederate soldiers whose mission behind enemy lines was to terrorize civilians in Indiana and Ohio and disrupt Union operations during the Civil War. The daring Confederates who survived a skirmish with Federal troops were shortly captured in Old Washington. The sight of Federal and Confederate cavalry clashing on the dusty streets of this small town must have been memorable. I don't think this sleepy little town has seen that much excitement since.

The hike from Old Washington to Seneca Lake went by fast. At Seneca Lake, I was greeted by Doug and Ethel Marie LeVasseur. They're my trail angels tonight. Doug maintains a section of the Buckeye Trail near his house, and he met up with me for the last five miles.

I'm spending the night at a cabin owned by the LeVasseurs. Doug's property is like a nature preserve. He's a conservationist and a naturalist with a special interest in bluebirds. He constructed a series of bird houses to encourage mating in a natural, safe environment. There's a nesting pair of bluebirds here now.

May 6: Day 48
The Feeling Was Unsettling

I hiked 19 miles to land owned by the American Electric Power (AEP) company.

Once again the route today was mainly on back, windy country roads except for a five-mile woods hike in Wolf Run State Park and a mile or so in AEP land. The forecast included rain. The terrain, as it has been for the past several days, is hilly and completely rural.

The Buckeye Trail passes a small granite marker commemorating the spot where the USS Shenandoah crashed in 1925, on its 57th flight. The USS Shenandoah was the first rigid airship, and the first of four airships to be commissioned for military use by the United States Navy in 1922. It was 680′ long, 79′ wide, and carried over two million cubic feet of helium. This lighter-than-air, reconnaissance aircraft crashed in a turbulent windstorm in Noble County. Out of a crew of 43, a few more than half the men survived. The airship broke into three pieces, two of which fell on what is now the Buckeye Trail.

Spring and summer in this part of Ohio are known for violent weather conditions. I thought about the crew of the ill-fated airship while I waited out the fury of an intense thunderstorm. I watched from inside the post office in Belle Valley while the wind and rain beat against the buildings and the pavement and lightning crashed overhead. It must have been a terrifying ride for the soldiers in the airship.

As soon as the rain let up, I headed for the AEP lands, sites of former strip mines. The company has spent millions of dollars reclaiming strip mined land in this part of Ohio and has opened them for recreation, which they call ReCreation land. It's a clever way to describe its land reclamation project. American Electric Power has taken 60,000 acres of former strip mined land and transformed it into an environmentally safe recreational area for the public. The company has planted over 63 million trees, created 380 campsites and 350 fishing lakes and ponds as well as horse, mountain bike, and hiking trails. The Buckeye Trail stretches for 22 miles on AEP land, one of the longest Buckeye Trail off-road sections. The next few days will be solid woods hiking.

The mile or so in AEP land was enjoyable until I entered a grassy field. The blue blazes just ended. I couldn't figure out which way to go. No trail in the grass, no blue blazes to follow, and lots of open strip mine area. I was lost. The feeling was unsettling, one that can make for a sleepless night. Nonetheless, I had food; I had water and dry clothes. I decided that the worry of the situation could wait until tomorrow. I set up camp and was in bed before the next rain shower arrived.

May 7: Day 49
A Day of Angst

I hiked 22 miles to almost the end of the AEP lands.

The route today was entirely in the woods on a footpath. It did not rain today, but my legs and feet were wet all day from the damp vegetation. It was a tough hike today.

The day awoke with sunshine. I knew as soon as I finished my relaxing cup of morning coffee, I needed to figure out where I was and how I got here. Being lost is always unsettling. The first step was to check the map. The map was of no help. I didn't recognize the surroundings. Was I on the trail and missed seeing a blaze? Something didn't feel right. The second step when lost is to backtrack. So, I backtracked to the haul road crossing to look for blue blazes. None were there. The third step is to get a GPS reading and check for a cell signal, using my smartphone and Google Maps to get a bird's eye view of the present location. I knew if I could spot landmarks and set my bearing, I could develop a plan. I saw that the haul road led to the main road. I started down the haul road and headed in the direction of the main road. A blue blaze! I gave a sigh of relief. From there on, the trail was very well marked on the AEP lands.

I didn't see other hikers today, but I did see turkey hunters, fishermen, and mushroom gatherers enjoying the weekend.

Coal is a cheap fuel and strip mining is a cheap way to harvest it. The process involves skimming away the upper layers of land. Hills, trees, and bushes are bulldozed, and all vegetation destroyed. The rock above the coal is broken down by explosives and removed in strips. The dirt, gravel, rock, and plant waste created are used to fill in the pits after the ore is extracted.

The waste needs to be leveled, covered with top soil, and replanted. The idea of reclamation is to restore the land to its prior state, but the top soil here is too thin to support trees and much of what I saw hasn't come back except for grasses and weeds. Unfortunately, it took some abusive environmental practices by coal mining companies to make this reclamation possible.

The problem is that grassy ground is uneven and hard to walk on. Plus, the continued rain has brought mounds of mud—slippery, slimy mud. Hiking the mud is tough, and it's wearing me out. To add to the problem, the traction of my quarter inch, grooved rubber on my Merrell Moab trail shoes are worn flat from 49 days of daily wear and almost 800 miles of hiking. I'm slipping. A hike is over when boots wear out or get lost or damaged. I'm ready to quit for the day.

Campsite, American Electric Power ReCreation Land

I discovered a remote campsite in a small pine forest at the edge of AEP lands. The angst of the day is starting to fade. I hear a turkey gobbling and a whippoorwill singing. The frogs are peeping, too. It is a fine night to be camping.

BUCKEYE
EST. 1959
TRAIL

CHAPTER 8
When the Going Gets Tough

May 8: Day 50
The Italian Scallion

I hiked 23 miles to Road Fork. I have now hiked 810 miles on the Buckeye Trail.

My day started early. Today I am tackling the Whipple Loop and need to prepare. I was up at 5:00 a.m. and on the trail by 6:10 a.m. in order to catch a shuttle ride from Doug LeVasseur at 7:00 a.m. I hiked a couple of miles to meet Doug. Doug shuttled me from the lower connector of the Whipple Loop to the upper connector in Belle Valley. Smaller loop trails (like the Little Loop) that lead off of a larger circular trail are logistically tricky because, at some point, they require backtracking. Doug's shuttle is saving me from repeating miles I've already hiked.

On the way north to Belle Valley, Doug asked me if I was interested in seeing Big Muskie. "Sure!" I answered, but hoped it wasn't the big fish on display at the Piedmont Lake Marina 100 miles behind me. Turns out, Big Muskie isn't a fish at all. Big Muskie is the largest single-bucket digger ever built. It's an artifact from the glory days of strip mining. The bucket is so large that the 100-member marching band of the local high school posed for a photo inside. The bucket is now on display at the Miner's Memorial Park, near McConnelsville. It's a reminder of the rich 200-year-old mining history of the area.

While in town, I loaded up on food. The Whipple Loop is remote, and I won't have a chance to resupply for six days. My hiker's appetite is in high gear, so I bought more food than a normal person can eat. I don't want to go hungry. I would have preferred to take hiker food. It's dehydrated, so it's lighter than packaged food and fresh food. Camping stores or department stores with a camping section sell hiker food. In this small town, however, I didn't have that option. I finally left town at 11:00 a.m. with a heavier than normal pack.

The next 21 miles were all on back roads. It was scenic and peaceful—only a dozen or so cars passed by all day. The fact that there is no mud, no fallen branches, no steep climbs gave me a much-needed relaxing hike. The fragrance of the spring blooms was heavy in the air, more so than past days. It smelled wonderful. The sun shone all day, and the temps were in the low 70s.

I arrived at Road Fork around 6:45 p.m. I have permission to camp at the Road Fork Baptist Church. The church is on the trail and has a bathroom for me to use. There's a cemetery a stone's throw away from my campsite. I sure hope it stays quiet over there tonight.

The Road Fork section, the Whipple section, and parts of the Belle Valley and Stockport sections comprise the Whipple Loop. It was added to the Buckeye Trail in 2005. It seems like it should be called the "Littler Loop" because, at 134.1 miles, it's much smaller than the Little Loop by almost 100 miles.

Loops on a circular trail seem redundant. In fact, no one I've talked to seems to know why the Whipple Loop exists, or the Little Loop for that matter. The Buckeye Trail is typically routed through areas that hold a particular point of interest or landscape. The unique sandstone bridge at Archer's Fork, for example, is in this section. My guess is that mapping a trail also has something to do with local politics and the economic benefit visitors bring to an area. The map calls the Whipple Loop the North Country Trail Connector. But it does not connect to the North Country Trail from what I can see.

This loop has another designation. It's affectionately called the "Stupid Loop." The reason? One story I heard was that when a hiker who had completed the entire circuit of the trail (and particularly prided herself on being a purist) found out that the Whipple Loop was added, she groused, "Do I have to do that stupid loop?" Stupid or not, I'll be going in a circle for a week or so before I start making westward progress home.

For the first time on this journey, I'll have a hiking partner for several days. Mike "Italian Scallion" Fanelli from the Dayton area is joining me.

In addition to being a caver like me, he's a long-distance hiker. I met Mike 20 years ago in a caving class through a mutual friend, Joe Windows. We live in the same town and know a lot of the same people, but we have never spent much time together.

So, I was very surprised when I got a call out of the blue from Mike ("Scallion" for short) to ask if he could come to hike with me. I told him that I appreciate that he had read my blog and wants to share my adventure, but honestly, I'm leery of hiking with a partner. I explained to Scallion that I've been on trail for two months now, and am trail hardened—got my trail legs, got my routine down, and move fast at 20 miles or more per day, wind, rain, or shine. I set my own pace and dictate my own schedule. Anyone asking to join me needs to keep up and adapt to my style. "Can you do it?" I asked him point blank. There was a moment of silence on the phone.

"Yes," he replied, "if I can nap in the afternoons."

I laughed. Who was it that said, "When the going gets tough, the tough take a nap"? That might actually be a good strategy for this part of the trail.

I'll be pleased to see Mike for another reason. He's bringing my spare pair of Merrell trail shoes that I bought before I started this journey. The new boots, as do the worn-out boots I'm wearing, have a 90-day, full-money back guarantee from the retailer. By my calculations, I'll be arriving home on day 88. You can bet I'll be making a trip to the store for my replacement pair.

It's bedtime now and a whippoorwill is being quite noisy. Anybody know how to get a whippoorwill to quiet down?

May 9: Day 51
Seeking Out Adventure

Scallion and I hiked 18 miles to the Ring Mill campsite in the Wayne National Forest.

Scallion and his wife, Sue, arrived at Road Fork Baptist Church just after 9:00 a.m. He greeted me with my new replacement boots and a plate of food from the hotel breakfast bar where he and Sue had spent the night. I scarfed down the food and put on my new boots. I was ready to go! Boots designed today require no break-in time. Sue offered to take the old pair back to Dayton for me.

About Scallion—he's older than I am by 13 years; he's trim, fit, and stands about my height at 6'. He loves caving like I do. Scallion is also an adventurer, like me. He backpacked the world for eight months in 2007 and 2008, visiting 35 countries. Other than that, I don't really know much about Scallion despite our long acquaintance.

The first thing I noticed was Scallion's small pack. He is carrying six days of food in a pack that is half the size and weight of mine. Scallion is an ultra-light weight backpacker and teaches backpacking clinics. Light weight backpackers value comfort on the trail over comfort in camp. He may not be carrying the camp amenities I enjoy (like two sleeping pads), but with less weight to tote, he can move faster and farther on the trail in a day.

The route today was all on scenic, back country roads. Having Scallion to talk to made the miles go by quicker. I had forgotten how nice it is to have someone to talk to. We shared hiking stories, caving stories, and family history. I told him about Maria. I did most of the talking. Scallion must think I'm a motor mouth. He sure is a good listener.

By afternoon, we were hot, tired, and thirsty. We stopped for a break under a shade tree in the front yard of a house. The owner was curious. He came over and sat down next to us on the grass. He had never heard of the Buckeye Trail and was surprised to know it came by his place. He gave us two bottles of chilled water to drink and filled our water bottles with tap water. I continue to be amazed at the kindness strangers have shown us on the trail.

We arrived at Ring Mill campsite and picnic area at 6:00 p.m. The Ring Mill campsite is along the Little Muskingum River. The picturesque tree-lined, gently flowing river was too inviting to pass up. Scallion took off his boots and waded in. He found clams in the river. These mollusks, plentiful in the Muskingum River, were once poached in huge numbers, and their lined, shiny interior sold to the pearl industry. We wondered if they were safe to eat.

The campsite is quiet. Nobody is here but us. We built a small campfire, lay on our pads, and gazed at the stars. By coincidence today is Joe's birthday. Our friend, Joe, passed away six years ago at the age of 71. I miss him and our friendship of 21 years. A guy like Joe Windows enters your life only once. You don't meet another person just like Joe. You don't have another friend just like Joe. I felt lucky to know him. He was full of life and vigor. He was my friend, my caving mentor, and like a dad to me. We backpacked together, caved together, and ventured into the unfamiliar to explore.

Joe claimed I once saved his life on a caving trip. It's a story I haven't told many people. The Hurricane Pit entrance of Pine Hill Cave in Kentucky requires the caver to rappel through a small opening to a larger room below. Joe went down first. As he descended through the hole, his helmet lodged in the opening, but he continued down the rope a short distance. In caving terms, it's known as a deadly "helmet hang." Joe was choking by the helmet chin strap as he dangled in the air. He couldn't speak. I sensed he was in trouble and reacted quickly. I whacked his helmet with my fist as hard as I could. His helmet dislodged; he gasped, and continued down the rope. He never forgot it.

As Scallion and I looked up at the stars, we felt that Joe, pleased that we were still seeking out adventure, was smiling down on us. Somehow we felt that Joe decided to join us for this journey.

May 10: Day 52
The Trail Was Fighting Back

Scallion and I hiked 10 miles just past SR-260. It took almost 10 hours. To put it mildly, the trail was a challenge today.

Leaving Ring Mill campsite began a 32-mile section of nearly all hiking in the woods. We were looking forward to this section in the Wayne National Forest, a part of Ohio we had never explored before. Wayne National Forest is unique in that it's the only national forest in Ohio and extends a quarter million acres across Ohio's hill country. National Forests are different from national parks in that use of natural resources for lumber and mining is allowed. Because of the remoteness, the hiking trail is also very primitive.

We soon got our first taste of the challenges ahead. While the blue blazes were plentiful, the trail along the Muskingum River was narrow, just a few inches in spots, and the waist-high grass made it hard to see.

The tall grass also obscured trip hazards like holes and limbs, making travel slow. Each foot placement was careful and deliberate.

After two or so miles along the river, we crossed a road and made the steep climb to the ridge. At some points, we had to use tree limbs or whatever we could find to pull ourselves up. It looked as if the only travelers through these knee-high weeds were deer. A number of downed limbs and blown-down trees were making the hiking difficult. The blazes for the most part were above the weeds and easy to spot. At least I knew we were headed in the right direction.

After our lunch break at Wilson Run Road, the price of travel went way up. In other words, things got worse. The blue blazes disappeared. We noticed instead that blue plastic diamonds were nailed to the trees. For the past 51 days, I've been following 2″ x 6″ blue, rectangle, Sherwin Williams Sweeping Blue #2408 blazes. Now, all of a sudden diamond-shaped, plastic markers are here? It took a close reading of the map and the trail descriptions before we figured out that the Buckeye Trail blazing had switched to diamonds. Yes, from a trail blazing perspective, plastic is more durable than paint, but it was a rough transition.

As the hike progressed, the plastic markers got fewer and fewer, and staying on the trail got harder and harder. Game trails intersected and crisscrossed through the weeds. Were we on the Buckeye Trail or a game trail? It was hard to tell. We got confused; we got lost. We tried calling the section supervisor a few times, but had no cell service. Before we realized it, we were off trail by a mile. Getting lost drained us of valuable time, energy, and morale.

We backtracked and devised a plan. At unmarked intersections, Scallion and I would split up and head in different directions to scout for trail markers. Whoever found a trail marker would blow two blasts on a whistle. The other person would respond with one whistle blast, then crash through the woods, bushwhacking to the spot, without wasting the time or the energy to backtrack. It was a good plan, but staying on the trail was a constant battle.

It was us against an unmaintained and poorly-marked section of trail, and the trail was fighting back. Trail markers were sparse. Weeds covered the trail. Blow downs were numerous. Climbing over, under, and through the blown-down trees was exhausting. Up climbs were steep; down climbs were steep. Drop-offs near the ledges were dangerous. We crawled. We climbed. We got scratched. We got bruised.

Scallion on a steep climb down, Wayne National Forest

We finally made it to SR-260. By now it was past 6:00 p.m. We had been on the trail since 8:00 a.m. and had only progressed ten miles. Our trail spanking had exhausted us.

Both of us are experienced hikers. We've hiked many trails and many miles. We know a bad section of trail when we see one. If this keeps up, we are going to declare this section impassable and walk on roads instead. We hiked another mile and set up camp.

Poor Scallion. He picked a fine section to join me. If he was discouraged, he never said. If he wanted to quit, he never said. I'm so glad to have a hiking partner. I am not sure I could have made it through this section solo. We were far better off together than I would've ever been alone.

May 11: Day 53
Thirst, Sweat, Exhaustion

We hiked 12 or so miles in the Whipple Section. It was hot and humid with temperatures rising to the mid 80s.

The trail had lots of straight ups and straight downs today. We could see where trail crews had constructed new trail and switchbacks to make hiking easier—not easy, just easier. The trail conditions went from bad to good to bad again. What started with blow downs, limbs, and high weeds magically morphed into a well-traveled dirt footpath in the woods once we passed Irish Run Road. This stretch is popular among mountain bikers who keep this particular part of the trail well maintained.

Like yesterday, blue diamonds replaced blue blazes as trail markings. Many of the plastic markers were on the ground instead of nailed to the tree. We first thought somebody was taking the markers off the tree and throwing them on the ground. But on closer inspection, we realized that the problem was that there was not enough space between the nail head and the bark to allow for the growth of the tree. It probably was fine for a year or two, but as the tree grew, it popped the markers off the nails and onto the ground. So, now the blue blazes were gone; the blue markers were gone and the trail was eroded. The only way to be sure we were going the right direction was to look for a broken marker lying among the weeds on the ground. It just made following the trail harder.

As we crossed into the Whipple section, the trail went back to rough going. More weeds knee to waist high, more blown down trees covering the trail. The vegetation was thick. The farther we went, the more overgrown the trail and the less marked. We got lost again. It was slow going, very physically demanding, and mentally exhausting.

We came out of the woods on a road, but within a few hundred feet, the trail reentered the woods, then emerged again on the road. We decided to skip the woods portion and stay on the road. The ups and downs, combined with temperatures in the 80s, wore us out.

The highlight of the day was a short detour to visit the sandstone cave and natural bridge on the Archer's Fork Loop. Both are good examples of sedimentary rock erosion. Geologic formations are not that common in Ohio, but there are about 80 natural bridges throughout the state. The formations at Archer's Fork are part of a sandstone bed that extends from the Appalachian foothills of Tennessee to Ohio. I've seen many natural bridges, each one unique, each one beautiful.

The day was characterized by thirst, sweat, exhaustion, and frustration with the overgrown trail. So when we noticed the neatly manicured grounds of a little country church—free of weeds and tall grass—just down the road, it looked like a fine, quiet place to camp. We pitched our tents on a flat area next to the church cemetery, high on the hill. We could see the Ohio River just a few miles away.

Campsite in cemetery at Deucher Baptist Memorial Church, Newport

We didn't realize that it was prayer meeting night until cars started to arrive. The sound of the piano and gospel singing filled the air. As we sat by our tents cooking supper and listening to praise songs at the end of a long day on the trail, my mind and body relaxed, and I could once again feel my love for this trail. Life doesn't get any better than this.

May 12: Day 54
The Experience was Unnerving

We hiked 14 miles to Sitka. Put an asterisk next to the mileage today. We decided to walk around the remaining six miles of trail.

I woke up this morning with a guilty conscience. Yesterday when we walked on the road to get to our camping spot at the church, we bypassed a short section of the Buckeye Trail. The purist hiker in me wanted to go back and mop it up. Scallion agreed but I'm sure the jungle-like conditions of yesterday's hike were still in his memory. If he was concerned, he didn't say. So, we backtracked the half mile, and entered the trail in the woods, hoping it was do-able with fresh eyes and renewed energy.

We followed a turn blaze and ended up in a field with an oil pump. The blazes ended. We were lost again and frustrated.

There's a suggestion on Buckeye Trail maps that acknowledges that parts of the trail, for whatever reason, are sometimes impassable and the hiker should be prepared to walk around those sections.

Others have reported similar difficulties on the Whipple Loop. Yes, walk around when the circumstance merits it, but for me, skipping trail is a hard mental adjustment. I want to say in good conscience I hiked the entire Buckeye Trail. At this point, though, I didn't feel like I had any good options; so, I once again decided to invoke the "walk around" caveat. We eventually found our way out to the road but not on the trail.

Just when I was hoping trail conditions would improve, the worst was about to come. The next section of trail entered a power line clearing. It was impassable. The weeds were chest high, mainly thorny rose bushes. The next part of the trail was again characterized by blow downs, fallen limbs, missing trail markers, and knee high weeds. We got lost. We found the trail again. We got lost again. There was no footpath to follow in this area. Hiking meant walking in weeds, around blown down trees, scouring for markers.

What compounded the level of physical demand is that southeast Ohio is exceptionally hilly. The hollows are rocky; the hills are rough, and the ridges, unlike the rolling symmetry of the Appalachian Mountain ridges, run in all different directions. The trail was frequently very steep, straight up or straight down.

Navigating around fallen trees wasn't an easy climb up and over the trunk. There were large limbs that extended directly from the trunk and branches that extended from the limbs. When the crown of the tree covered the trail, we battled limbs, branches, and thick foliage. If we slipped on wet bark or in mud, we slid into the tree or worse, down a steep embankment.

In one section, the only way to get around a blown down tree was to walk over a former garbage dump. We walked on broken glass and through piles of discarded household items, tires, and building materials. In another area, falling trees had knocked down a power line. We had to assume the line was live. From a safety perspective, we shouldn't have gone near it, let alone climb over it, but it was blocking the trail in two places. Scallion and I stood there a minute trying to decide what to do. The electric fence episode near Defiance would be nothing compared to the high-voltage shock the power line would deliver. Power lines are not insulated with rubber like power cords, and the result of contact is serious injury or death. But climbing over was the only option to stay on course.

Stupid or not, we decided to stay on course even if it meant crossing the power line. We crossed safely, but the experience was unnerving. Obviously, this part of the trail has not been maintained for years. It was just too difficult and dangerous to continue.

Should we get off the trail? I consulted with Scallion. Over the past three days, I have come to respect his opinion, his wisdom, and his calm demeanor. "Andy, this is your hike. You do what you think needs to be done" was his advice. "I'm here to support you." He trusted my judgment, and I was gratified. The decision to invoke the "walk around" caveat was up to me. We walked on roads around the remaining six miles of woods trail.

Road walking was much easier, and we were making good time. But we were hot, tired, thirsty, sweaty, and smelly. We spotted a farmer

Downed powerline and trees over the trail, Wayne National Forest

sitting on his front porch in the shade of a large veranda and stopped to ask for water. We credit what happened next to trail magic.

Eric not only gave us cold water to drink, but invited us to rest. His wife, Debbie, served us soda and sandwiches. We met an important member of the family—Pancake. He likes to chase cars. Eric is certain one day he'll find Pancake flattened like a pancake on the road.

Eric and Debbie seemed truly interested in what we are doing and why. They enjoyed hearing about the adventure of doing what we love and promoting the Buckeye Trail at the same time.

We talked about other things, too, including the gas and oil boom in the area. The Marcellus Shale under the ground holds large deposits of natural gas. Landowners are being approached by speculators and oil companies to sign gas leases. There are promises of big money for landowners once drilling starts. Unfortunately, some farmers, unaware of the market value of the trillions of cubic feet of natural gas below ground and pressured by hungry energy companies, signed away rights for only a few thousand dollars. Scallion and I heard firsthand what issues affect farmers on this side of Ohio.

We thanked our hosts for the good food and interesting conversation. I gave Eric my Buckeye Trail business card. My Buckeye Trail support family just grew by two.

About a mile before our intended campsite for the night, we encountered more trail magic. We came upon an enclosed picnic shelter, a camper trailer, and an outhouse. The property owner happened to be driving by and gave us permission to camp. He even filled our water bottles at his house. We appreciated our second instance of Ohio hospitality today, and our weary feet were glad to be done for the day.

May 13: Day 55
Making It Out of the Stupid Loop Alive

Scallion and I hiked 13 miles to the town of Whipple. We were glad to leave the unmaintained parts of the Whipple Loop behind.

We got up at 6:00 a.m. this morning. The plan was to get an early start. This was my idea. However, we lounged around our campsite drinking coffee and talking until almost 9:00 a.m. and did not get an early start. This was my idea.

The miles went by fast today—easy compared to the last few days. We enjoyed the road walking, confident we were on the trail, unlike the last few days of painstaking guesswork. By 12:45 p.m. we were in the small town of Whipple. We rewarded ourselves for making it out of the Whipple Loop with burgers, fries, and drinks from a small convenience store.

By trail standards, Scallion is an excellent hiking partner. Some hikers have only one criterion for a good hiking partner: someone who carries beer and is willing to share. My compatible hiking partner, however, has to have three things: strong performance, even temperament, and good hiking habits. Scallion has all three. He is well prepared, self-sufficient, hardy, and experienced. His knowledge and experience comes from hiking the Appalachian Trail end-to-end, the Long Trail, 800 miles of hiking on the Pacific Crest Trail, decades of knowledge as a Boy Scout leader, and having recently spent eight months traveling the globe, visiting 52 countries, carrying nothing more than a backpack. Scallion is also easy to be with and flexible. Some hikers care strictly about laying down miles. Miles are important to Scallion, but he also enjoys seeing the sights and chatting with locals like I do. We share similar hiking habits. We hike the same pace, take breaks when necessary, and only quit for the day when we're tired. Scallion would have preferred to get an early start on the trail each day, but waited patiently while I enjoyed my two cups of morning coffee and updated the blog before we hit the trail. Good hiking partners are like that.

My plan is to take two zero days in a row. After twelve straight days of hiking, I need a break. It's also been 12 straight days since I've seen Maria. My plan with Maria is to rendezvous this afternoon at a cabin near Seneca Lake and relax for the weekend. Sunday is a milestone birthday for me.

I feel a little guilty abandoning Scallion for the weekend and spending it with Maria. But he understands love and romance. He and Sue met when they were just teenagers. Mike worked at the concession stand at the pool the summer of his junior year in high school, and Sue was a regular customer. Her dad dropped her off at the pool whenever he played at the local golf club. That was 46 years ago. It was a summer love that lasted a lifetime.

I hope my new love lasts a lifetime, too. My shuttle driver arrived on schedule at 1:00 p.m. to take me to a cabin in the woods for a long weekend with Maria.

May 14 & 15: Days 56 & 57
Maria Is Special

I took two days off from hiking and spent the days relaxing with Maria in a cabin in a remote part of southeast Ohio.

This is the 28th day I have known Maria. I have seen her on all or part of 13 of those days. It's kind of amazing when I consider that I'm in the middle of a long-distance hike on the Buckeye Trail. Long-distance hikers don't usually find love on the trail. Besides the fact that hikers are dirty, smelly, and hairy, they're not really looking for love. Hikers are in love with the trail. In all of my years as a long-distance hiker, I have never fallen in love on the trail. Nor has anyone ever fallen in love with me.

This was love at first sight. Maria is petite and pretty. But, what is it that triggers an instant romantic love for a stranger? Some say the attraction is chemical, triggered by smell or sight or a perceived sense of familiarity. I just know that when I looked into Maria's warm brown eyes, and she returned my smile, I felt my heart jump.

But what did Maria see in me that first encounter? Did she think I was handsome? Did she notice my friendly and happy personality? My honest disposition? Maybe it was my spirit of adventure and my passion for hiking. Whatever the reason, love blossomed. Our time together these past two days has been sweet.

This weekend was special for another reason. Sunday was a milestone day for me. I celebrated making 50 revolutions around the sun. Maria and I cooked steaks on the grill, ate salad, fresh green beans, birthday cake and ice cream, and enjoyed the peacefulness of the woods and each other's company.

I feel so content today. I'm with Maria; I'm hiking my first 1,000 miler-plus thru-hike. I'm so appreciative of life, and the many kind people who are helping me for no other reason than they believe in my journey and want to be a part of it.

However, when a person turns a half a century old, he realizes that he has fewer days ahead than were behind. I guess it's normal to think about missed opportunities and trails not taken. I have often wondered if I've missed something in life by never marrying. I can't really explain why I've never married. Maybe I'm afraid to commit to a long-term relationship. Maybe I love hiking, adventure, and the thrill of uncertainty too much. Maybe I'm too independent.

Whatever the past reasons, could it be time to settle down? I have great expectations for the future whatever it brings.

I resume hiking on the Whipple Loop on Monday. I'm glad that Scallion has decided to join me for a second week. He has been hanging out in Stockport that last few days. Scallion didn't mind that I wanted to be alone with Maria. He understands how love blossoms whether or not a person is looking, whether or not the time is convenient, whether or not the circumstance is suitable, whether or not there's a master plan. He knows that Maria is special. Mother Nature has a couple of cool and rainy days in store for us.

May 16: Day 58
The Man Behind the Curtain

Scallion and I hiked 20 miles from the town of Whipple to the Morgan County line. We didn't start hiking until noon and were finished by 7:00 p.m. The route today was on back roads.

After two days of rest and relaxation, I was refreshed and anxious to continue the journey. Maria and I picked up Scallion near the AEP lands. He took a county-funded shuttle from Stockport to the edge of the county. As long as he stayed within the county, his shuttle fare was only $2 even though it was a 30-mile ride. It saved us a 50-minute drive to get him. Maria drove us back to Whipple so we could pick up the trail and then left for Cleveland.

The area is remote, sparsely populated, wooded, and hilly. The ridges look as if they had been strip mined. Luckily, the temperatures were in the mid-50s with a slight breeze. This is perfect for hiking. The sky was overcast with rain in the forecast, but it never rained. We clipped away the miles, thankful the 80-degree weather from last week wasn't following us. Hot weather puts an extra strain on the hiker that cooler weather doesn't. In cooler weather, body heat radiates away from the body and into the air. In hot weather, especially during periods of high humidity when the air is saturated with moisture, body heat is absorbed back into the body, jump starting the body's cooling system. You sweat more; you drink more to stay cool, but if you can't replace the four liters of fluid and electrolytes you're losing throughout the day, you're prone to heat exhaustion, dehydration, and heat stroke.

The cooler weather and the long stretch of road walking invited conversation. I wanted to ask Scallion's advice about something. I'm on the verge of a major decision—giving up my career. I've spent the last 27 years of my work life in the business world. I consider myself a hard-working, dedicated professional. I completed an MBA years ago to advance my career. My plan was to work for another 12 years. But I'm feeling burned out, discouraged with the corporate world, and generally unhappy.

Could I survive without a good paying job and the benefits? I have been focused nearly my entire life on making money. When I was young, my dad praised my entrepreneurship when my brothers and I sold penny firecrackers to the neighborhood kids for a nickel. At age 13, I had a paper route. In junior high, I trapped muskrats in a nearby stream to sell their fur to vendors for $5. Sometimes I even skinned them myself to fetch a higher price. My mom says that I still have the first dollar I ever earned.

Scallion retired at 52 as an engineer. He never worked another day and never looked back. I asked Mike what he thought I should do. Instead of giving me advice, he hit with me tough questions. Do I want to make more money? Do I need more money? Will more money make me happier? Do I enjoy sitting in a cubicle? Do I have the time to enjoy the money I'm making when I'm sitting in a cubicle? Am I willing to stay on a path that sacrifices happiness for money?

His arguments were convincing. I could swing the adjustment financially, but I was still perplexed. "What will I *do with myself* if I leave my career in IT?"

He just looked at me and said, "You're doing it."

It struck me that maybe Mike was the man behind the curtain telling me that I already had the answer I was looking for. Along Keith Creek, we climbed up an embankment and found a flat, grassy area near a small pond. We set up camp and were in bed by 9:00 p.m., hiker's midnight. I have a lot to think about.

Campsite outside of Stockport

May 17: Day 59
Life Is Just too Short

We hiked 21 miles to the town of Stockport, finishing the Whipple Loop. I crossed the 850 mile mark today. I am so glad to be finished with the Whipple Loop. Yes, it deserves its nickname of the Stupid Loop.

It rained last night, and when the sun came up, it was still raining. Neither Scallion nor I was in any hurry to leave our cozy tents. I heated some water for coffee by placing my stove outside my tent at arm's reach. I lounged in my tent, pleased with the effort. It finally quit raining around 9:00 a.m., and we packed up.

The route today was on back country, often unpaved roads. The only things out here were Scallion, a few cars, and me. The area is remote, rural, sparsely populated, and economically depressed. There are a lot of abandoned buildings. Homes, barns, rusty trailers, shacks from mining days are in various states of neglect and decay.

Half way through the hike, it started raining. It rained for almost three hours. It was a cold, steady rain that soaks even the best-protected hiker.

At the crossroads in Hackney, we sat on a covered porch of an old storefront loaded with junk to escape the rain. An intoxicated old fellow drove up and shouted out to us.

"Do you have permission to be here?" He sounded angry.

"We're Buckeye Trail hikers," I shouted back, hoping he would excuse the fact that we were trespassing. He stayed quiet which made us uneasy. After a few moments, he spoke again.

"Well, don't put any dimes in the pop machine. It's broken." His friendly warning about the broken pop machine put us at ease. The fellow went on to explain that Scallion looks exactly like the owner of the old store. The fellow was just ribbing since he thought he knew us.

Nine miles outside of Stockport, we decided to forego camping and book a room at the Stockport Mill Inn. Being wet and cold was wearing us out. Besides, I hadn't been feeling right all day.

This morning, I received an e-mail informing me that a high school friend of mine, Josie Gill, had died of breast cancer. Josie was my date for our junior year prom—the only prom I went to. I remember driving the family car over to her house, meeting her parents, and nervously pinning a corsage on her. I wasn't her first choice for prom. The guy she liked had asked somebody else, and a friend suggested I ask Josie. I was thrilled that she said, "Yes." It wasn't a romantic evening, but it was a fun evening.

I'm sad that she's gone. There was a special spot in my heart for Josie because she went to prom with me. We didn't date in high school; I hadn't seen her in years, and we hadn't stayed in touch, but I always thought if I ever got the chance, I'd ask her out on a date. I had imagined that maybe we'd be one of those high school sweethearts who'd fall in love after 20 years.

Now that will never happen. Death has a way of marking the passage of time. I'm grieving for Josie, but I'm also grieving for me because I'm getting old. Life is just too short.

Scallion and I made it to Stockport by 7:00 p.m. We were cold, wet and tired. We unpacked and hung our wet tents, clothes, and gear on make-shift drying racks—hooks, towel bars, shower rod, bed posts, door knobs, and/or any suitable vertical structure available in the room. We ate supper at a pizza place, took showers, and were in bed by hiker's midnight. More rain is expected tomorrow.

BUCKEYE
EST. 1959
TRAIL

CHAPTER 9

An Inspired Commitment to the Trail

May 18: Day 60
Enjoying a Simple Life

Scallion and I hiked 25 miles. We took the opportunity to slackpack.

We awoke again to rain. But this time we were in a nice inn instead of our tents. All of our gear had dried out nicely.

We arranged for a 9:30 a.m. shuttle pickup with the Morgan County Transit Service. Our driver dropped us off 25 trail miles (17 road miles) away, a few miles past Shew's Orchard Farm. Our plan is to hike back to Stockport and spend a second night in the Mill B&B. The shuttle cost us $2 each. This is an incredible deal for a 75-minute taxi ride. The route again today was on back country roads.

By 10:15 a.m., the rain had stopped, and the sun was out. We moved quickly without the full weight of our packs on our back. We stripped down to shorts and shirts in no time.

We saw two young Amish boys driving a horse-drawn cart carrying logs to a small saw mill. The highest population of Amish in the United States lives in Ohio. I think it's around 60,000. The ones I've seen on my journey live a traditional Amish lifestyle. They travel by horse and buggy, hang wash on a line to dry, dress in plain clothes, don't use tractors for farming, and generally live a simple life. Chesterhill, where we took our lunch break today, and Stockport were first settled by the Quakers.

After the boys dropped off their logs, they rode slowly past us to check us out. Then, they turned around and rode past us again. It was clear they were sizing us up. We smiled at each other both times, but we didn't speak. Usually what happens when locals are curious is that they stop to chat. I enjoy answering questions and telling them about the Buckeye Trail. That didn't happen today because I don't think Amish boys are allowed to initiate conversations with the "English," as they call us. The boys were definitely intrigued, though. They probably don't see many travelers on foot carrying only the bare necessities on their backs and enjoying a life even simpler than their own.

As we made our way down the trail, we were reminded what it means to be deep in the hills and hollows of southeast Ohio. Only the dirt roads reach way back into the hollows or "hollers" as the locals call them. Some of the back roads did not have bridges at the stream crossings. We forded or hopped across seven stream crossings. The water was fast moving, but it was only ankle deep. Crossing streams without bridges may not be a problem for cars or carriages, but it can't be good for the wildlife in the stream.

Fording the creek on Newburn Road, near Chesterhill

We arrived back in Stockport about 8:30 p.m. We rewarded ourselves by calling in a pizza order from the trail. We picked it up, went to the inn, and got off our feet for the day. Another great day of hiking.

May 19: Day 61
The Good Kind of Crazy

Scallion and I hiked 17 miles to the dam at Burr Oak State Park. It was a long day. I am now in the New Straitsville section which is map 18 of 26.

For the third straight day, the Morgan County Transit service picked us up in Stockton and dropped us near the trail head. The route today was almost all in the woods on trails except for a couple of miles of road walking.

We said goodbye to Stockport. Modern Stockport is a sleepy little village of about 500 people, but this one-time wild riverboat town has a rich history. Stockport has survived Indian raids, Confederate Army raids, the railroad era, the steamboat era, industrialization, the temperance movement, World War I, and the Great Depression. One of the last remnants of Stockport's thriving past is the Stockport Mill. The once functioning grist mill now solely generates electricity.

It was another day of hiking the wooded, hilly terrain of southeast Ohio. We started with a steep climb up Stump Road. The pain and effort it took to reach the top was rewarded with a panoramic view of the Hocking River Valley. The meandering Hocking was an important passageway to runaway slaves fleeing north on the Underground Railroad.

Soon the trail turned into the woods in the Wayne National Forest. It's described as a patchwork of national land because all quarter-million acres are not contiguous. The park is spread across nearly 12 counties and so is divided into three units to make supervision manageable. Scallion and I are about to enter the Athens unit, the one farthest west. We're both apprehensive about woods walking again in the forest. We expected to find missing trail markers and fallen trees blocking our path. We were wrong. The trail was very well maintained, easy to follow, and the inclines were graded. The trail through Burr Oak State Park was also "easy" miles.

In Burr Oak, the trail passed close to Buckeye Cave. It's a recessed sandstone cave with rock walls on three sides and a waterfall. The cavers in us wanted to see a cave we've never seen before. So, we hiked down and took a coffee break to check it out.

All day I'd been debating whether or not to attend the Buckeye Trail Association (BTA) annual meeting that would be held in just two days. Andrew Bashaw, the executive director of the BTA and the regional officer of the North Country Trail Association, offered to pluck me off the trail if I wanted to attend. The annual meeting is the largest gathering of BTA members. I've been a lifetime member of the BTA since 2000, but I've never once attended an annual meeting. Honestly, the words "annual meeting" alone were enough to keep me away. The problem for me now was that it is going to be held at The Barn at Tappan Lake, a two-hour drive north. Plus, I had zero-ed at the barn three weeks before and going back to Tappan Lake would feel like going backward, at least mentally. I was only 500 miles from home and really wanted to push forward. Besides, I had already told Andrew, "no."

But Andrew wanted me to attend because the Buckeye Trail community is reading my daily blog and want to meet this guy from Dayton who is solo circuiting the trail as a thru-hike. Scallion also encouraged me to attend by pointing out that I've become the face of the Buckeye Trail to people all throughout Ohio who have never heard of the trail. He reminded me that the BTA has become my support community. Members who have helped me will be attending, as well as section supervisors and trail maintainers. It would be an opportunity to thank them.

The realization that I *needed* to attend (not just *should* attend) came over me like a jolt of lightning. I stood straight up from the rock where I was seated and announced, "Scallion, I'm going to the annual meeting!"

Now my problem was that I had to reach Andrew to tell him that I had decided to change my plans. Incredibly, I had cell service in the cave, and more incredibly, the call connected to Andrew.

Scallion just smiled at me and called my eleventh-hour decision "the divine intervention of Joe Windows." Andrew will pick me up tomorrow.

It rained the last five miles of the hike. It was a steady drizzle that soaked us. We were running out of daylight from the numerous breaks

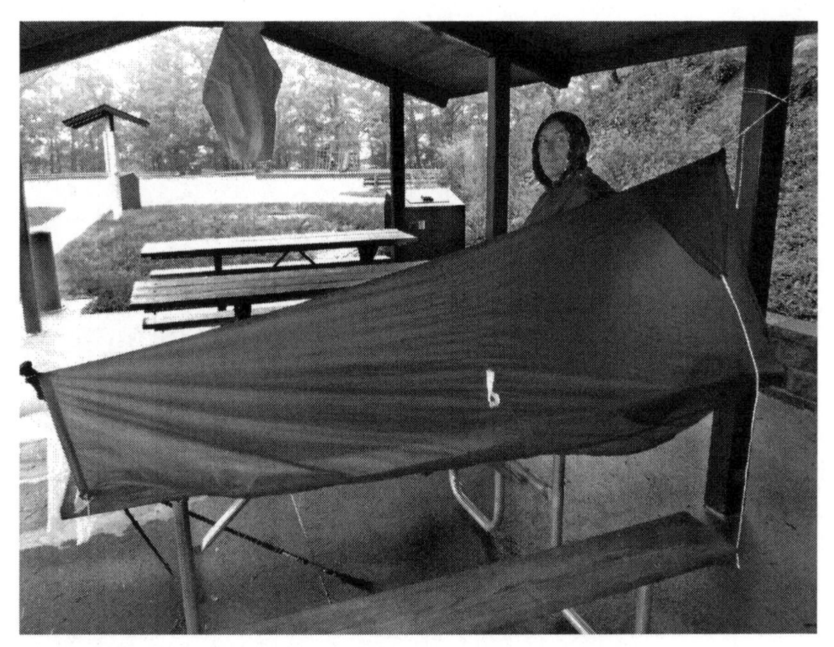

Scallion camping on a picnic table at Tom Jenkins Dam, Burr Oak State Park

we had taken during the day, and the wet, muddy trail was slowing us down. We arrived at the Tom Jenkins Dam at 8:45 p.m. We spotted a picnic shelter, water fountain, restroom, and trash can. The finest amenities of outdoor living! We set up camp under the picnic shelter, happy to be out of the rain.

Even though we hiked in a steady rain in almost complete darkness through muddy, hilly, and wet terrain, we had a great time—something only a long-distance hiker can appreciate. People think we are either a special breed or we are crazy. I will end today's post with a motto of long-distance hikers: "We are out here because we are not all there." If the interpretation of the expression means that long-distance hikers are crazy for happily tolerating the misery of the elements, sore knees and feet, a high-calorie, borderline nutritional diet, and long periods of solitude, then "yes," we are crazy. But it's a good kind of crazy, the right kind.

May 20: Day 62
I Shook My Friend's Hand and Said Goodbye

Scallion and I hiked 11 miles to Murray City.

The rain stopped sometime after midnight. We awoke to a damp and foggy morning. We took our time getting packed and hit the trail around 9:00 a.m.

After a short walk down the Burr Oak dam access road, we entered the woods. The woods were still wet and muddy from the rain. The trail was well maintained and easy to follow. We came across three guys on an ATV coming down the trail. One was carrying a shovel. They claimed they were from the gas company checking for gas leaks. "Smell any gas?" one fellow asked.

"No," we replied. Their story smelled to us. We suspected they were in the Wayne National Forest to dig something or plant something. The woods back here are fairly dense, a good cover for questionable behavior. If something illegal is going on, it won't be the first time. I heard that in 1926, prohibition officers conducted a raid and destroyed a 50-gallon still and 10 barrels of mash back in these woods. Maybe history will repeat itself.

We arrived in Murray City at 1:30 p.m. in time to meet our shuttle drivers. Scallion was off to Zaleski State Forest to join his scout group from Centerville for a weekend of backpacking, and I was going to Andrew Bashaw's house in Glouster for a shower, laundry, supper, and a ride to Tappan Lake.

It was time for Scallion and me to part ways. His presence and encouragement these last 11 days have made the journey richer. The days in the Whipple Loop were a test of my ability to go the distance on this hike. They were not fun hiking days. I had said from the beginning that when this journey wasn't fun anymore, I'd quit and head home. I may have done exactly that if it hadn't have been for the companionship of Scallion. The longer I continue, the stronger my desire is to finish. I'm too invested in this journey now to just quit because it's hard. I have more miles behind than I have ahead. I'm now stronger—physically, mentally, emotionally—and more committed to walking home via the Buckeye Trail than ever, thanks, in part, to Scallion. I shook my friend's hand and said goodbye.

Andrew, his wife, Claudia, and toddler, Adelaide, and I piled into the family car after supper and drove to the Buckeye Trail Association Annual Meeting at the Barn in Harrison County. We arrived with just enough daylight left to set up our tents.

I met lots of volunteers and hikers. I chatted with Poppie, Couscous, Pioneer Spirit, and BTA Geek. All were circuit hikers who had completed the trail or were working on completing the trail. I knew these guys by their trail names, but had never met them in person, only conversed with them via the Trail Talk discussion board on the Buckeye Trail Association website. All were also following my blog. All were happy to finally meet me. The conversation was friendly and social. It was the usual hiker talk—asking questions about particular areas and sharing memorable stories.

One Buckeye Trail Association member, Jackie Hale, was so impressed with my journey that he offered to buy me a six-pack of beer in town. I was delighted. I enjoy a cold beer at the end of a good day. I would have bought my own, but I'm a pedestrian these days, and by foot, town is a good hour away. At the mention of the offer, I had assumed that my kind benefactor would hop in his car and drive to town and that within 30 minutes, I'd have a cold six-pack of beer in my hands. I was looking forward to the gift. He did leave right away. But it was hours before he came back, and empty-handed to boot. He was, needless to say, apologetic (and I suspect, feeling a little guilty for consuming my beer before he returned).

May 21: Day 63
A Strong Sense of Belonging

Today was the annual meeting of the Buckeye Trail Association (BTA), held at the BTA Barn on Tappan Lake.

The meeting started promptly at 9:00 a.m. Officers and staff members gave brief reports on finances, trail maintenance, trail updates and issues, followed by the annual election of board of trustee members.

After lunch, we had our choice of field trips: a hike, a pontoon boat ride on Lake Tappan, or a visit to a local railroad museum. I chose the most relaxing option, the pontoon boat ride. Twelve of us plus two crew members loaded into the boat. We spent a pleasant two hours on the lake. I was the only one who opted for a swim. At 70°, the water was a bit chilly, but it felt good.

After dinner, Paul Stutzman, author of the book *Hiking Through*, gave a presentation. He hiked the entire Appalachian Trail in 2008 to grieve the death of his wife of 32 years. He turned his grief into an adventure.

I thought his presentation was timely. I know from experience that the trail is a perfect place to reconcile loss. Just as emotional baggage slows a person down in life, it slows a hiker down on the trail. In a physically demanding environment like the Appalachian Trail, a hiker is forced to push past emotional pain in order to endure the trail's challenges.

My dad died in November 2009, and my job came to an end three months later. These losses sent my internal compass spinning. The following June, I headed back to the Appalachian Trail to seek out the solitude I needed to work through my sadness. Those two months I spent on the trail helped me to sort through good memories, bad memories, and regrets—what to keep, what to shed. By the time I had reached Katahdin, the northern terminus, the emotional burden had lifted. The saying on the Appalachian Trail is that the trail provides. It did for me; it did for Paul Stutzman and many others like us.

All long-distance hikers hike for a reason—to exercise, to heal from grief, or to escape something, whether it's everyday routine, work, or a relationship. As one Appalachian Trail hiker told me, he and his buddies hike to escape wives, ex-wives, and future wives. Paul's story is what my friend, Tagalong, calls a "hell-to-redemption" tale, a tale of hope for a life after loss.

This morning, at Poppie's request, I spoke a few words to the group about my hike on the Buckeye Trail. As I stood there in front of the 40 or 50 members present, I felt a sudden surge of emotion. I expressed my gratitude to those who've helped me. I confessed my embarrassment that I've been a life-time member since 2000 but had never taken the time to attend an annual meeting or worse, hike the trail because I thought it wouldn't be interesting or exciting. I apologized to fellow members that, before this journey, I had never given the Buckeye Trail a chance.

I'm also overwhelmed with the sense of what it means to be a member of the Buckeye Trail community. This community is a group of like-minded people from all walks of life from all parts of Ohio (and beyond) who choose to protect, preserve, and advance a specific geographic area for the purpose of promoting Ohio's past and present. The Buckeye Trail is both educational and recreational, and members watch out for and care for each other.

The community has provided food, shelter, gear, and companionship when I needed it. I've come to love the trail and the community—my trail family. So I made an important decision today. I'd like to serve on the board of trustees if given the opportunity. It'll mean working without pay, driving long distances for meetings and events, and engaging in fund raising. Actually, I'm not sure what it all entails, but I'm willing to make the commitment. I want to contribute. I want to give back.

After Paul's presentation, a group of us went outside to enjoy each other's company around the campfire. I feel such a strong sense of belonging here. What a good day it's been.

May 22: Day 64
Little Cities of the Black Diamonds

I hiked nine miles to Shawnee. Miles today were easy, despite the steep hills.

Andrew, Claudia, Adelaide, and I were on the road home by mid-morning. By mid-afternoon, I was in Murray City and back on the Buckeye Trail.

The first half was on back roads, and the rest of the hike was in the woods in the Wayne National Forest. To my relief, the Wayne National Forest trail was well marked and in good shape. One reason is that All Terrain Vehicles (ATVs) are permitted on this part of the trail. I am not a fan of ATVs on hiking trails, but they are doing a good job of keeping the trail packed down without doing major damage to the treadway.

At Tecumseh Lake, I took a side trail into the town of Shawnee, population 655. As is Murray City and New Straitsville, Shawnee is a former coal mining town, and is located in the Little Cities of the Black Diamonds region in southeast Ohio. "Black Diamonds" is another term for coal. Fifty communities spread over three counties sprouted in the Hocking Valley Coalfield in the late 19th and early 20th centuries during the boom. It was Ohio's version of the California goal rush.

The coal industry went bust when coal was no longer the largest source of energy and mining became less dependent on human labor. With nothing to fill the void, local economies decayed. It shows. Buildings on the main street of Shawnee are empty and deteriorating. It has a ghost town feel.

Shawnee is an interesting place, though. It's built on a hillside. The buildings on the main street remind me of an Old West ghost town with their empty, abandoned, and dilapidated store fronts on the main street.

For a small town, Shawnee is packed with history, too. The Little Cities of Black Diamonds building is part museum and part library. It tells the sad story of the life of the coal miners in the Hocking Valley. The coal industry was unregulated and workers were heavily exploited. Not far from here in New Straitsville, angry mine workers set a fire in retaliation against mine owners in 1884. Eventually, mine workers in Ohio were able to unionize, unlike miners in neighboring West Virginia, in part thanks to the efforts of miners from this area. This area is the birthplace of the Knights of Labor movement, a precursor to the formation of the United Mine Workers union and perhaps one reason the Shawnee Historic district is listed in the National Parks Service's National Register of Historic Places.

Unfortunately, the New Straitville's mine fire still burns deeply underground. I can see no visible smoke or odors from the fire, but it's a reminder of turbulent times in these now peaceful communities.

I am spending the night in Harrop House. The Harrop family lived here from 1890–1990. The house itself is 120 years old. Today it serves as the headquarters of the Buckeye Trail Association and Andrew Bashaw's office. Long-distance hikers, no matter if their affiliation is North Country Trail, American Discovery Trail, or Buckeye Trail, are welcomed here. It's old and creaky, but the upstairs bedrooms have everything a hiker needs: a bed, a shower, a bathroom, and a computer. I hope it's not haunted.

May 23: Day 65
The Worst Is Mud

I hiked 22 miles. Bruce "Poppie" Purdy joined me. The first part of the day is on road; the second part is in the woods in Wayne National Forest.

I'm pleased that Poppie (a stranger to me before last weekend's Buckeye Trail Association's annual meeting) drove from the Columbus area to join me on the trail today. Poppie is Pop (to his son), Poppie (to his grandchildren), a Vietnam veteran, a retired high school industrial arts teacher, and a former scout master.

Poppie is also a Buckeye Trail circuit hiker and leads circuit hikes. A circuit hiker is someone who hikes the trail in sections, not continuously, and not necessarily in sequence. It's the most convenient way to hike the entire trail. A circuit hiker can day hike on the weekends, with gear or without. He or she can eat in a nice restaurant at the end of the day, car camp or sleep in a Motel Six, be a fair weather hiker and choose the season, the temperature, and, if really flexible, the forecast. The drawback is that circuit hiking requires patience and time. Hiking one weekend a month, averaging 25 miles per weekend (like most circuit hikers do), a hiker completes the entire trail in about five years. Poppie is on the five-year plan. I, on the other hand, am on the 90-day plan. However one does it, finishing 1,444 miles of trail is an accomplishment no matter how long it takes.

Today, Poppie and I decided to hike counterclockwise, from Logan back to Shawnee, so I can spend another night in Shawnee. I always feel good when I know I have a place to sleep.

We waited out the morning storm and hit the trail by 11:30 a.m. I'm not a meteorologist and know little about jet streams and La Niña, but having lived outside most of the last 65 days, I can say the weather in Ohio this spring has been wild. Ohioans joke, "If you don't like the weather, wait ten minutes, and it will change." This weather, however, goes beyond normal for Ohio. Apparently, weather all over the United States has been extreme—either epic flooding or record drought. I could use a little drought right now.

Poppie

By mid-afternoon, we entered Wayne National Forest. We hit the horse trails first. In general, hikers detest bridle trails. Granted, horse trails are easy to follow and add valuable miles to the Buckeye Trail. But they're designed for horses, not hikers. Unlike a two-legged traveler, a horse can easily manage steep inclines and descents without switchbacks. For the hiker, though, straight ups and downs aren't the worst part. The worst is mud.

Mud makes trails very vulnerable. When a trail is wet, hikers walk into it, punching in two or so inches. With a much greater mass and force, horses punch down even further. When the mud dries, cup-sized holes in the trail remain. When it rains again, the water doesn't flow off the trail into the woods like it should; it fills these cups, holding the water. The more traffic on the treadway, the worse the problem becomes. The mud, the incline, the dips, the holes, the lumps, and the slime slowed us down. We may as well have been hiking in wet concrete. It was that difficult.

Once off the muddy bridle path and into the woods, we soon faced a new problem. The blue blazes, if they were there, were not visible. We got lost twice. Both times, we got confused when the trail intersected forest roads. Both times were frustrating experiences. Between us, Poppie and I have hiked almost 2,000 miles of Buckeye Trail. We know how to follow the trail, we know how to read maps, and we know what to look for. But we ended up making wrong turns.

The second time we got lost, we got separated. Poppie found the trail again by walking down a township road. I found the trail again by using Google Maps on my phone and back tracking. He called me. We met back up and continued hiking. Thank goodness for cell phones, Google Maps, and cell coverage.

This is the last of my hiking in the Wayne National Forest on the Buckeye Trail. Unfortunately, my first and last impressions are not that great.

Poppie got a shuttle back to his car at 8:30 p.m. I continued hiking to Shawnee with the last of the remaining daylight. I made a side trip to the Marathon convenience store for pizza and beer. I arrived back at the Harrop House at 9:30 p.m., just before another bad storm hit. I ate supper, showered, crawled into bed, and listened to the rain pound on the roof. It's been a long day.

May 24: Day 66
Blaze Bandits

I hiked 16 miles to the Hocking State Forest.

The more tired I am, the slower come the miles. Today, they came slowly. I'm worn out from yesterday's trail spanking. I stopped at Lake Logan campground and made a cup of coffee. It helped a bit. I had a pleasant pick-me-up when I found an unopened bottle of malted adult beverage at a campsite clearing. I suspect my trail angels were the Guy brothers who are the trail maintainers for this section. As much as I appreciated the thought, it was too early in the day to enjoy, so I left the trail magic untouched for the next hiker.

The trail was on-again, off-again road walking, meandering through the woods. Each time the trail made a turn into the woods, a feeling of dread washed over me like a wave. The woods walking was a replay of the bad memory of the last two weeks. Once again, I crawled over downed tree trunks, branches and limbs that littered the trail. Locating blazes was again a scavenger hunt. In one section, somebody had tried to "black blaze" the trail by painting over some of the blue blazes with purple paint. Covering up a blaze prevents hikers from finding the trail. Why would anyone want to purposefully confuse a hiker? A disgruntled land owner? A tree hugger who wants to keep people out of the woods? These blaze bandits weren't too smart. They didn't notice that the blue blazes were on both sides of the tree. Blazing opposite sides of a tree is the way the maintainers mark the trail for hikers approaching from opposite directions. When I realized the vandal missed the blue blazes on the opposite side of the tree, navigation got easier.

To add to my challenges, the muddy trail followed me through stretches of woods like a pest. It oozed up and over my boots and settled down inside. Wet, muddy boots are double the misery. Wet boots equal wet feet and caked mud equals reduced traction and grip on the trail. Muddy boots don't dry out overnight either. Tonight as part of my camp chores, I'll remove as much mud as possible. Beating a boot against a rock or hard surface may seem like a good idea, but it breaks down the boot support. Instead, I'll carefully clean the crevices of the tread with a stick, then stuff the inside with newspaper to absorb as much moisture as possible. Drying shoes by the fire helps, but it's too hot today to build a fire. The newspaper will help, but my boots won't be entirely dry by morning. I'll repeat the process tomorrow and for as many days as needed. I've put on wet boots almost every day of this hike.

As I made my way along the small and windy Wildcat Hollow Road, I began to see sandstone outcroppings and hemlock trees. It was very pretty. I soon entered Hocking State Forest.

The change was dramatic. It was wide, not muddy, not weedy, easy to follow, and no downed trees. The trail followed the contour of the land along a stream instead of going up and down. The trees were tall, majestic hemlocks whose pine needles, not low vines, not saplings, not weeds, covered the floor of the forest like a blanket. It was so pristine and so beautiful that it looked like a movie set. I felt like I had died and gone to hiker Heaven, the hiker Garden of Eden, the hiker Promised Land. For the first time in days, I relaxed. I put hiking on autopilot and let my mind wander. I had forgotten how enjoyable this kind of hiking was. I guess you have to experience the bad in order to appreciate the good.

I found a comfortable campsite near a stream and a small waterfall. I had hoped to hike farther, but the campsite was too pretty to pass up. I have the woods all to myself tonight.

May 25: Day 67
Grandma Gatewood

I hiked 20 miles to the Pretty Run property in Vinton County owned by the Buckeye Trail Association. I crossed the 1,000 mile mark!

I woke up this morning refreshed and savoring the thought that when I crossed the 1,000-mile point yesterday, I had set a new personal record in terms of miles and days on the trail. Before this hike, my record was two months, three days, 840 miles. Another first for me if I finish is that this will be the longest thru-hike I've ever completed.

Yes, if I finish. There was never a firm plan to complete the entire trail. I always make it a point to avoid grand announcements of any future significant hiking accomplishments that haven't yet transpired.

Over the years, I've noticed a correlation between hikers who make grand announcements about hiking the Appalachian Trail end-to-end and success rate. About two million hikers hike some part of the Appalachian Trail every year. Some even quit a job to take on the five-to-seven month end-to-end journey from the southern terminus, Springer Mountain, Georgia to Mt. Katahdin, Maine the northern terminus. Only about 25% of the hikers who plan a thru-hike each year ever complete it.

I think hikers who make grand announcements have self-doubt and by making their goals public, it commits them to a plan about which they have doubts. It seems the more excited about a thru-hike hikers are, the more people they tell, the less likely it is for them to finish. The hiker who keeps his goals to himself generally does succeed.

Whether or not I finish this hike in the next few weeks, all I know is that, with each mile I walk, I'm that much closer to home, and the closer I get, the more determined I am to finish.

That fine stretch of easy hiking in Hocking State Forest ended when I entered the woods again after a pleasant road walk. I quickly got my mind back to the trail when hiker's heaven soon turned to hiker's reality.

The pretty hike up to the cliff line lined with sandstone boulders, caves, and ledges was eclipsed by the condition of the footpath. The reason for the sudden change of trail condition wasn't hard to figure out. I was on a shared horse-hiker pathway. Whenever a footpath is shared by horses and hikers, the hikers are the ones who get the losing end of the deal. Every hoof print makes an indentation which creates a small puddle. The small puddles make for one long stretch of muddy trail. I sludged along, forced to slow my pace in order to give my shoes better traction on the slippery surface.

It was a relief to finally reach the peaceful haven of the majestic rock formations, falls, and caves of Hocking Hills State Park. Hocking Hills has been a favorite all-year round hiking destination for me for the past 35 years and for many others. Lazy summer days have drawn millions of visitors each year into the cool, peaceful recesses of the caves and the refreshing spray of the waterfalls since the 1870s. In the cold of winter, snow-covered ledges and icy stalagmites and stalactites transform the caves into a winter wonderland of beauty.

The trail passes above Upper Falls where a monument to Emma "Grandma" Gatewood is located. This Ohio native hiked the entire Appalachian Trail three times starting at the age of 67. She is credited with being the first female to solo thru-hike the Appalachian Trail. Her backpack was a drawstring sack slung over her shoulder; her hiking boots, a pair of Keds tennis shoes. A shower curtain was her rain gear; a walking stick, her trekking poles. This stretch of the trail is named in her honor not only because she's a legend in Appalachian Trail hiking circles, but also because she is considered to be one of the pioneers of

Upper Falls, Hocking Hills State Park

Ash Cave, Hocking Hills State Park

the Buckeye Trail. The Appalachian Trail inspired the creation of the Buckeye Trail. Grandma Gatewood hoped that one day the Buckeye Trail would connect to the Appalachian Trail. Hence, the blue color of the blaze, which on the Appalachian Trail indicates a connector trail. Grandma Gatewood also liked the idea of a powder blue trail blaze because the color stood out against the background of the forest.

As enjoyable as my respite in Hocking Hills was, now it's 6:00 p.m. and I still have eight miles to go. I pounded out the miles in two-and-a-half hours. I arrived at the Rice cabin on the Pretty Run property and set up camp. Byron Guy is supposed to meet me here with my trekking pole replacement parts. He did not show, or I am in the wrong place. We will sort this out tomorrow.

May 26: Day 68
Hiking in the Age of Technology

I hiked 16 miles to Tar Hollow State Park.

It rained last night, but I managed to stay dry. That is, until I started hiking. The tall grass and weeds were still wet from the rain. I quickly got soaked from the knees down. This seems to happen every day. It's impossible to keep my boots dry.

I came across Byron Guy this morning. He had camped out on the Pretty Run property last night, too, but at a different location. We chatted a bit in the sun and ate a couple of day-old McDonald's chicken sandwiches. Byron is going to spend the day doing trail maintenance on the Pretty Run property. He had the replacement parts for my Black Diamond trekking poles. My poles are as good as new now.

I've been hiking with borrowed trekking poles for the last 70 miles. One of my Black Diamond, aluminum-alloy, cork-handled, $85 trekking poles snapped in half. I'm not surprised or disappointed. My poles work hard. I would've fallen many times on these muddy hills if it hadn't been for the stabilizing force of my trekking poles. It's natural for poles to wear out from the force and weight transfer.

Technology has sure changed the hiking experience. On my first long-distance hike in 1989, I made due with a stout wooden stick. If it broke on the trail, finding another to replace it was not a problem.

Smartphones didn't exist then either. I called my mom from pay phones which were usually next to busy roads or noisy intersections. I had to rely on day hikers for news and weather reports. My first pair of boots had hard soles and leather uppers. Boots today are actually trail shoes—low cut, reinforced tennis shoes, very comfortable with little or no break-in time. My tent in the 1980s was bulky and heavy, and my attire was an old shirt and cut-off jeans. Today, tents are nylon with light-weight carbon fiber poles, and clothing is designed to protect against rain and wick away sweat. Technology has made hiking safer and more comfortable. So, even though it took several phone calls and several e-mails to Black Diamond to order replacement parts, I happily put up with a little inconvenience.

I'm glad to have my own poles for the steep climbs on the trail today. The trail took me up a road hollow and high over a ridge. The steeper the climb became, the narrower the road, and the fewer the houses and farms until finally the road, the houses, and farms disappeared. I felt like I was summiting a mountain. I can see why this area was slow to settle in the 1800s. The land is too steep and rutted to farm. Oak and hickory used to cover these ridges. Now it's been clear cut for lumber.

Around 6:00 p.m., I was met by trail angels. Connie and Mike Snyder host just about every long-distance hiker who comes through on the Buckeye Trail or American Discovery Trail. I got a much needed shower, a delicious meal, and a bed to sleep in.

Connie first learned about hikers when she was postmaster in Londonderry. Hikers would mail resupply packages to her post office. It's common practice for hikers to mail items they need on the trail to themselves via "general delivery." When hikers would come to retrieve their packages, Connie got acquainted with them. Connie and Mike have a scrap book full of photos and letters from the hikers they have hosted over the past ten years. I happily posed for a scrapbook picture.

May 27: Day 69
Grandpa Andrew J. Niekamp

I hiked 19 miles to Scioto State Forest.

I'm slackpacking today and for the next three days thanks to Mike and Connie, my trail angels. They dropped me off at Tar Hollow at 9:00 a.m. I forgot to mention yesterday that this area got its name from the tar taken from Pitch Pine trees that grew here. Tar was an important household commodity for early settlers.

Today was a combination of woods walking and road walking, both gravel and paved. One of the oddest things I saw today was near Blue Lick Road. The area had been clear cut recently, and the loggers removed all the trees except for the ones with the blue blazes marking the Buckeye Trail. The loggers either knew what the blue blazes meant or mistakenly thought the blue marks meant the trees should be saved. The only trees standing had blue blazes on them. It was so easy to follow. Scallion and I could have used a few less trees in the Wayne National Forest.

As I walked on the road after lunch, a young fellow in a Jeep stopped and asked if I was hiking the Buckeye Trail. He offered to drive me down the road to where the trail enters the woods. It was a kind offer, but it would mean skipping miles. No purist likes to skip miles. When I hiked the Appalachian Trail in 1990 in Shenandoah National Park, I

Field near Lickskillet

skipped six miles of trail. It was fun to jump ahead and get a taste of every challenge the trail had to offer. But I felt guilty and later had to mop up the missed miles. It was a lot harder logistically, financially, and psychologically to make-up miles, and I vowed never to skip miles again if I could help it. I declined but thanked him.

I crossed to the west of US-35 and over the Scioto River. I entered Scioto State Forest. I'm near Chillicothe now. I have family history tied to this place. During World War I, this area was home to Camp Sherman, an Army training camp. When my grandfather, Andrew J. Niekamp, whose namesake I carry, was drafted into the army at age 26, he was stationed at Camp Sherman. Camp Sherman was built in 1917 to quarter soldiers and horses being shipped overseas in support of the war. At its peak, Camp Sherman housed 40,000 soldiers and 12,000 horses and mules.

Tragically, a flu epidemic swept through camp in the fall of 1918. According to Niekamp family records, 1,177 servicemen died in one month. The number of soldiers who perished was so high that a theatre in downtown Chillicothe was converted into a temporary morgue. The bodies were stacked up like cordwood, waiting to be shipped back to their respective families. When a stable hand died of the flu at Camp Sherman, my grandfather was promoted to sergeant and took charge of the stables. This twist of fate allowed my grandfather to remain stateside for the remainder of the war. It meant a lot to me to see the remnants of the original Camp Sherman, knowing that my Grandpa was a part of its history.

At 6:15 p.m., I arrived at a designated spot in the state forest. Mike and Connie arrived to pick me up. We went out to dinner in Piketon and made a quick trip to Walmart for me to resupply. Then it was off to bed.

BUCKEYE
EST. 1959
TRAIL

CHAPTER 10

Putting My Commitment to the Test

May 28: Day 70
A Burst of Energy and Determination

I hiked 26 miles through the Scioto State Forest and across US-23 to Nipgen.

Parts of the trail today are easy, maintained and graded. Parts are rugged and muddy. The ridges and valleys are a constant up and down, designed for horses, not hikers. The green among the trees is pretty—Dutchman's breeches, blue phlox, ferns, mosses. The damp, moist, shady parts of the trail make it a good place to hunt for morel mushrooms in the spring.

After crossing US-23, the trail crossed into private property, through a short stretch of high grass, through a rusty gate and a pile of abandoned construction materials. I was dreading the next stretch. But to my surprise and excitement, I saw Jeff Yoest standing down by the creek. Jeff is a trail maintainer from Columbus. Jeff had heard I was coming, drove out to this section, and weed whacked the trail ahead of me. He even had a can of paint to mark a few areas on the trail. In my enthusiasm, I asked him to paint a small blue blaze on my hat. He did.

For the rest of the day, the trail followed back roads. I was relieved to be hiking on roads again. It made for much faster and easier hiking.

The day was hot, and I was running low on water. The map showed I would reach Mapleberry Farms in a couple of miles. Mapleberry Farms is a family-run business that produces maple syrup. I called ahead to see if I could stop for some water. Nobody answered, so I left a message. Nobody was home when I arrived. I left one of my Buckeye Trail cards in the door and moved on, hoping to come across another water source soon.

About 30 minutes down the road, I spotted a car coming toward me with an arm waving out the driver's side window holding my Buckeye Trail card. It was Gale Rickey, the owner of Mapleberry Farms. He had arrived home, listened to my message and drove out to find me. He handed me a cold, refreshing quart of ice water. To see me standing by the side of the road on a warm spring day chatting with Gale, a passerby would have thought we were old friends. I was once again gratified by the interest, kindness, and support of a stranger.

At 7:30 p.m., I arrived in the small town of Nipgen on SR-772. Mike and Connie drove out to pick me up. It was a 27-mile drive for them. We ate dinner in Bainbridge, toured Chillicothe, and then headed back to Richmond Dale.

The ups and downs today were tiring, but I feel good. My feet are in auto-mode. They have toughened with each mile. I have my trail legs. It helped that my Buckeye Trail family helped me to slackpack. But the big morale boost was that when I crossed to the west of US-23 today, I knew I was officially back in southwest Ohio, the final leg of this four-cornered trail that I call home. Wilbur and Orville, I can't wait to see you again! I feel like a horse does when it's headed for the barn. I have a burst of energy and determination knowing that the goal is within reach. I know I can finish this hike!

May 29: Day 71
Buckeye Trail Blowdown Blues

I hiked 18 miles in Pike State Forest.

Gently rolling hills are replacing the rugged ridges. The rainy weather has made the trail lush and green, but the garlic mustard, the honeysuckle, the low growing thorny bushes, and the weeds covering the path are full of mosquitoes, gnats, and ticks. Pulling off ticks has become a daily routine. The overgrowth is also covering the blazes, making it impossible to stay on the blue blazes. I wandered off the Buckeye Trail several times today.

Blown down trees over the trail, Pike State Forest

But the worst part of the trail today is the fallen trees. Winter and spring have brought unusually harsh weather in Ohio. The fierce storms have downed many trees. So many are covering the trail that I'm crawling over, under, around, and through a tree every 50 yards or so. I'm sweating bullets in this 90-degree weather. Not a fun hike.

If I were a song writer, I would write a ballad about fallen trees over the Buckeye Trail. This sad song would be sung in exasperation like the coal miner from years ago who worked all day in the mines. No matter how hard he worked, there was still more coal to be mined the next day. No matter how many fallen down trees I hike through, over or around in a day, there are still more waiting for me tomorrow—another and another and another.

I wonder if the song writer, Merle Travis, would mind if I tweaked the lyrics of his song *16 Tons*. How does the "Buckeye Trail Blowdown Blues" sound for a title? Wish I had Tennessee Ernie Ford's deep, rich voice.

You wrestle sixteen blow downs, and what do you get?
You get beat up, bruised and soaked in sweat.
St. Peter don't call me, 'cause I can't go.
There's more blue blazes in O-hio.

I didn't realize that I was so good at writing lyrics. The fact is I really don't feel like singing at all. I'm getting more and more discouraged with each fallen tree.

I tried to give myself a pep talk. As the crow flies, I am about 60–70 miles from home, only an hour and a half by car. By trail, I have only 334 miles to go on a 1,444 mile-trail. I can do these miles in my sleep, I told myself.

The pep talk wasn't working. For the past 70 days, I've lived like a nomad. Every day, I migrate to a new place, find a place to eat/sleep and move on. This lifestyle has kept me focused and on the trail for the last 1,110 miles. It would be easy to assume that after 1,110 miles, hiking is easy now. This is not the case.

The continuous physical exertion and the daily uncertainty are wearing on me. Even though I'm close to home, there are still many more miles to hike. I'm distracting myself with thoughts of home and life after the trail. Now, more than ever, the challenge of the hike has become a mental game.

After almost 11 hours on the trail, I was glad to see Connie and Mike and relieved to be out of the woods.

May 30: Day 72
My Spirit Finally Broke

I hiked 14 miles to Fort Hill State Memorial. Put an asterisk next to today's miles as I had to bypass some sections. It was the worst day I've had on the Buckeye Trail.

Connie and Mike dropped me off at 11:30 a.m. They hosted me for four nights. They drove me around so I could slackpack—all told about 175 miles. They gave me a bed to sleep in, fed me, and allowed me to use their computer, shower, and laundry. Connie packed me a lunch each day. I felt so well-cared for.

I waved goodbye to my two wonderful trail angels and turned toward the trail. Almost immediately, my heart sank. A feeling of despair washed over me. The trail appeared abandoned. I could barely see 20 yards down trail in front of me. "Oh, no," I thought, "what am I getting into?"

Overgrown trail, Pike State Forest

I pushed through the waist-high and shoulder-high weeds that were growing across the trail or what I could see of the trail. The overgrowth scratched my legs, shoulders, arms, and hands. I couldn't see below my knees. The weeds covered my feet. It was hard to tell where I was stepping or on what. I tripped and stumbled as my feet became entangled in low-growing prickly weeds. Each step meant fresh scratches. The temperatures soared as the day wore on. My body sweat was attracting gnats and mosquitoes.

I was in full combat mode. When I wasn't battling weeds and overgrowth, I was maneuvering my way around trees and limbs strewn across the path. Unlike the trees from weeks past, these weren't blown down by an act of nature. Someone had selectively logged a few trees and left the tops covering the trail. They were hard and dangerous to navigate.

I wandered off the trail and got lost. I backtracked. I lost the trail again. I backtracked. I missed a turn when the trail changed direction in an unexpected place. I backtracked. A few times, the blazes were so faded or obscure I missed them. Each time, I backtracked.

Once when I missed a turn, I ended up at an Amish farm. I could tell it was an Amish farm because it had the longest clothes line full of clothes I had ever seen. An Amish lady was holding a baby and hanging wash. In desperation, I approached to ask for directions. She looked up from the clothes basket, unalarmed as if it were an everyday event to give directions to bearded strangers who wandered onto her farm. She told me to backtrack which I did. I found the turn I missed.

I came to a spot where the blue blazes went in two directions. A faded sign by a logging company said the trail was rerouted in this area. I chose the wrong set of blazes and got lost. I backtracked and followed the second set. The trail disappeared into the woods. Whoever blazed this route spaced out the blazes too far. I got lost a few more times. To me this part of the trail looked abandoned.

Pushing through the thick on an uncertain footpath was physically exhausting. Navigating with few blazes was mentally exhausting. I was expending twice the physical energy and three times the mental energy. I seriously started to worry about getting lost. Then it happened.

My spirit finally broke. Hiking the trail in this condition was too tough on me. I realized that I wasn't hiking the trail. I was fighting it instead. I came to the Buckeye Trail to hike it not fight it. As much as I have tried to maintain a positive attitude, the truth is, the trail has been in bad condition for the last week. And I can no longer continue.

I am lost and mad. Heck, I am mad at myself for thinking I could do this. For the first time, I feel like quitting.

Hiking is not a spectator sport. I know that, but there are certain things you can predict and certain things you come to expect. Some things in nature, for example, are predictable. Every hiker knows that there will be mosquitoes, ticks, bird poop, and bad weather. That's nature. Every hiker knows that there will also be blisters, broken gear, body odor, and, at some point, boredom. The hiker, in turn, expects certain things from the trail. He or she expects the trail to be adequately marked and navigable. If the trail is not marked and is not navigable, the trail lets you down. What do you do when hiking becomes combat? How do you know when it's time to quit or to go on?

I needed to blow off some steam. So, I found a high knoll and got out my smartphone. In frustration, I wrote an email to the Buckeye Trail Association executive director, board president, state trail coordinator and a few trustees. I explained how poorly maintained the trail was and pleaded action. They need to know how bad the trail had gotten. I am just one of a series of hikers who hike on the Buckeye Trail in southern Ohio and encounter these conditions. Some hikers quit in frustration and never come back, I explained.

Even though I knew no one would come to my rescue today, writing the e-mail helped to calm me down. I took a deep breath and decided to take Winston Churchill's advice on tenacity: "When you're going through hell, keep going." I resumed hiking.

I finally got to a road. I was whipped physically and mentally. It took almost four hours to go three miles. I was so disappointed.

I decided to walk to Fort Hill on roads instead of taking trails. There was no way I was going back into the woods in this section. The route by road was slightly longer than by trail but it was easier. My head was still spinning from what I had just come through.

I got to Fort Hill and took a break under the picnic shelter. It was shaded and breezy. The nearby stream looked like a good spot to cool my burning heels in the 90° temperatures. It was like a little bit of heaven. I decided to set up my tent under the picnic shelter and crash for the night. Nobody bothered me there. I was glad. I needed to be out of the woods in a place where I felt secure. I lay in my tent and waited for the peace that comes with the night to lull me to sleep.

May 31: Day 73
The Serpent Mound and Mythical Power

I hiked 21 miles to the town of Peebles.

It was a brutally hot day of hiking. The temperature reached 90° with a "feels like" of 98. The route today was all on roads except for four miles.

The night was quiet, and I woke up refreshed, but still feeling unsettled about the hike yesterday. The situation yesterday wasn't impossible. I wasn't hurt. I had water, food, and my cell phone worked. I eventually found my way out. I've been in tighter spots on the trail before, and know what that feels like. One such experience has stuck with me for 20 years.

John Rausch, the cave guide, my buddy Joe Windows and I, just a rookie caver at the time, were in Pine Hill Cave, in Rockcastle County, Kentucky. Pine Hill Cave is a gem of waterfalls, 40′ to 100′ dome caverns throughout, and canyons above and below. The trip was to be a straight shot, "go in one hole and out the other."

Caving is dangerous. Caves are damp, musty smelling, and usually muddy. A cave system is a maze of passageways that can be a lengthy meander or a dead end. Narrow passageways, low ceilings, crevices, holes, drop offs, falling rock are constant dangers. The landscape is monotone and its nuances hard to remember. A caver has to be alert to the dangers of hypothermia and vigilant to stay warm, dry, and hydrated.

Soon after rappelling from the entrance above to the passage way below, it was apparent to Joe and me that John was lost. He had no idea where we were. That meant we were lost. It's hard to describe the feeling of being lost in a cave. It might be days before anyone would come to look for us. John realized the seriousness of the situation. Fear started to creep in. Exhausted and weak, John broke down emotionally and was unable to continue.

Suddenly, we heard voices below. Luckily, another group was in the cave that day, but we were too high up in the cave system and couldn't see them. Joe and I took charge. We scurried along the trail, desperately trying to catch up to the sound of the voices. Finally, we got the attention of the last caver in the group.

"Hey!" I called out. "We're lost up here. Do you know where we are?"

A voice from out of the darkness replied, "No! I can't help you. My team is too far ahead. I need to keep moving, or I'll be lost myself. Good luck!" We needed more than luck.

Joe and I devised a plan. We would follow the direction of the other cavers in hopes of finding an access down. It was clear to us that they were on an established path. Good plan/bad plan? It was the only plan we had, but it was enough to deflect the panic that follows fear when lost in a cave. We kept moving until we found an access to the path below with a place to attach the descending equipment. One by one, we rappelled down. We were exhausted, but greatly relieved to see familiar pathways and rock formations. We were too mentally and physically drained to carry the equipment out, so we gladly abandoned it and made our way to the opening. I remember the tremendous sense of relief when the sunlight hit my face that day. The feeling was similar yesterday when I walked out of the woods.

I was still thinking about yesterday's walk through Ohio's jungle, when I came upon the famed Serpent Mound. It was built and used by the Adena and Fort Ancient Indians and believed to be constructed in 1,000 AD. Its tail is curled, its mouth open, and its body undulates in waves along the contours of the land. It's beautiful.

Native Americans held ceremonies there to honor the powerful serpent spirit. They believed for whatever reason that this place was magical.

Strength is derived from hardship. The mythical Ninja warrior believed that only after he had endured great hardships could he derive supernatural powers from the earth. It was strange, but I sensed a connection to this place. Yesterday, I was nearly defeated by the trail. Today, I feel strong and confident. I wondered if it was a coincidence that I came through the hardest part of this journey at this place. I stood there several minutes to absorb my thoughts and feelings. It was inspiring to think that the ancient Indians walked the same ground I had just walked and endured similar hardships to what I had just endured from this land. Perhaps I am deriving the power I need to continue this journey from this ancient earthen serpent.

Serpent Mound, Adams County

My next challenge was to get supper and find a place to spend the night. I headed toward the pizza place where there was a good chance I could find both. In a small town like Peebles, the pizza parlor is the place to get good food, news, and local information. Sure enough, someone there knew where I could get a place to camp with access to a restroom and fresh water. She made a call and within minutes, Larry, a town councilman, picked me up and drove me back to his house to let me camp in his yard.

June 1: Day 74
Family, Friends, and an Infected Toe

I hiked 20 miles to Wamsley. Most of the route today was on roads.

I woke up to another hot day. I caught a warm breeze along the farm fields. A warm breeze is better than no breeze. I lost the blazes and the trail in a field of waist-high weeds near Mineral Springs. For me, getting lost is such a morale killer.

The day wasn't all bad, though. I ascended steeply to a ridge and soon entered Davis Memorial State Nature Preserve. The landscape of the small nature preserve with its gray dolomite cliffs and heavily wooded trail certainly isn't out of place in these southwest Ohio hills. But it is unique. Pre-glacial plant life thrives here and a six-mile fault line is a reminder of the tremendous force of pressurized heat trapped beneath the surface.

I took a side trail and stopped for a break at Cedar Fork Cave. I got a long drink from the cold spring water pouring from an underground stream at the entrance of the cave. I dropped my Gatorade and my hydration pouch into the water to cool down and poked around a bit at the entrance of the cave. It was too tiny to go much farther than the entrance.

I made it to Wamsley by 6:00 p.m. I was happy to see Mom and Jim in Wamsley. I hadn't seen them since the day they dropped me off at Deeds Point on March 20. They made the two-hour trip from Dayton to spend a few days with me in a cabin in Shawnee State Park. Mom made dinner for me. It felt good to sit down to a home-cooked meal with family.

After dinner, my mom inspected my toe. My little toe has been bothering me for the past couple of days. It was painful when I had my shoes off but not so much when I was hiking. Foot and toe pain are routine on the trail, so I just ignored it. The toe was infected, my mom pointed out, no doubt caused by weeks of wearing wet and muddy shoes.

Long-distance hikers need to be prepared to endure physical trauma. Blisters, poison ivy/oak, sunburn, tick bites, swarming insects can slow a hiker down. The serious ailments like dehydration, giardia, hyponatremia, hypothermia, infection, and/or norovirus can stop a hike altogether.

An infected toe can become gangrenous if untreated. During World War I, foot infection, also called trench foot, was a death sentence for many Allied soldiers who lived in abysmal trench conditions. Unfortunately, it was common in the wet, unsanitary conditions.

I needed to see a doctor about my toe. Luckily, a good friend of mine from my caving days, Brian Saul, had lived in Portsmouth for many years and was familiar with the area. I contacted him to ask if he knew of a good family doctor in town. He passed the phone to Sheryl, his wife. I had forgotten that she was an emergency room physician. I described my problem and e-mailed her a few digital photos of my toe. She confirmed that it was infected and phoned in a prescription for me for an antibiotic. It was an unexpected dose of good fortune—trail magic—and I was very grateful.

Tomorrow is going to be a zero day. I need to let this toe heal a bit before I start hiking again. I can use a day of rest and a day out of this heat.

June 2: Day 75
My Mom

Today was a zero mile day. Mom, Jim, and I are staying in a cabin at Shawnee State Park.

It felt good to rest for a day after eleven consecutive days of hiking. My mom and I drove into Portsmouth. We went to Walmart to shop for groceries and resupply items, and to pick up my antibiotic prescription. I will be on antibiotics for five days to fight my toe infection. I got a haircut while in town, my second on this journey. Typically, long-distance hikers prefer an unkempt, shaggy appearance. It represents time spent on the trail. It's a symbol of seniority among hikers. On the Buckeye Trail, however, it was more important to have more of a clean-cut appearance as I'm still an ambassador of the Buckeye Trail. I washed my backpack, too. It smelled worse than I did.

We toured the Portsmouth floodwall murals. The floodwall murals are a colorful, larger-than-life, pictorial history of Portsmouth that cover 2,000 feet of the wall. One of the panels is a picture of the devastating 1937 flood which ravaged not only Portsmouth with rain and high water, but also every town and city along the Ohio River. The floodwalls were built by the United States Army Corps of Engineers after that flood. Someone must have thought these towering concrete barriers created a natural canvas to tell the history of Portsmouth. I felt like a casual time traveler as we strolled along the 50-some murals that compose the wall.

It was good to spend the day with my mom. I love my mom a lot. She's a good mom and has always been my biggest cheerleader. She (with my dad) raised five kids, had a successful career as an educator, earned a masters degree in night school, and still managed to make us kids her top priority. She kept us on top of chores, catechism, music lessons, odd jobs around the neighborhood, school work, sports, and extracurricular activities. My mom ran an orderly household, and we learned a lot with rules and through example. I got my mom's German thriftiness, stubbornness, punctuality trait, her work ethic, her independence, and her emotional strength.

My mom is not a hiker, but I attribute my love for the outdoors to her. My mom encouraged me and my three brothers to play outside. In a noisy household with four boys, playing outside was sometimes more of a directive than an option. When we boys were outside, it was a wonderful way to discover nature.

My siblings and I grew up in a developing community in the 1960s, one that was transitioning from a rural to a suburban neighborhood. It offered me and my brothers plenty of freedom to explore in the fields, the woods, and the creeks.

And my mom let us be kids. If she minded that we carried home toads and snakes to adopt as pets and caterpillars to watch spin a cocoon, she never said. We caught butterflies and put turtles in old shoeboxes to

Jim and Mom

show off to the neighborhood kids. We played in the creek and overturned rocks to find salamanders, crayfish, minnows, and fish. I remember it as being one of my first tastes of freedom away from the watchful eye of adults. I think that's when I developed my sense of adventure.

As a kid, playing in the woods was a way to escape the daily routine. Going to school, church, basketball practice, band practice, piano lessons, doing chores or homework can be stressful for kids.

Being outside for long periods of time was my stress relief. And years later, that's still true for me. It's part of the reason I hike. It's a way to reset mentally.

June 3: Day 76
Two Words: Up-Down

I hiked 20 miles to Shawnee State Forest.

My infected toe felt much better today after taking the antibiotics and getting a day of rest. The pain and discomfort from two days ago is gone. My toe is good enough to walk on.

The first part of the route today was on roads. I had a close encounter just past Wamsley on Mt. Unger Road. There's a house with at least 30 vicious dogs in the yard. They looked like strays. When the dogs saw me approaching, they began to bark, growl, and howl in chorus. The noise of the dogs was deafening.

Most were securely chained to a pole, but it didn't stop them from running after me at full speed only to be suddenly yanked back by the collar. Not all of the dogs were chained and several ran out in the road to charge me. They barked, circled, and snarled, baring teeth. I stepped up my pace and kept them at bay with my poles. It's common to see free-running farm dogs in the country, but encountering so many mean dogs at once was unsettling. This property is a potential safety hazard to hikers.

The rest of my day would have been uneventful, but I missed a turn from a gravel road to a dirt road and ended up walking two miles off trail before I realized it. There were no blazes to indicate a turn. To make matters worse, I mistook the white blazes on the poles and trees as faded blue Buckeye Trail blazes. These were indeed white blazes and indicated an alternate route around Shawnee State Forest.

Wamsley Church, Adams County

The gravel road soon became a dirt road and eventually came to an end. I sighed deeply and headed the direction I thought I should be going. I found myself walking across a farm meadow when I saw an ATV coming toward me.

The owner, Bob Hill, stopped me to find out what I was doing on his property. I explained that I needed to get back on the Buckeye Trail and asked if he could give me directions. To my happiness, Bob knew of an abandoned township road that connects to the trail. He said all I needed to do was walk through a hayfield, through the woods, then keep walking until I came into the backyard of some private property, walk down the driveway, cross the creek, and then I'd be on the road the Buckeye Trail follows.

I nodded my head in acknowledgment knowing that the reroute was going to put me on the trail ahead of the location of the missed turn. I mentally calculated about a mile, mile and a half of missed trail. If I followed Bob's directions, I would be breaking the continuous steps principle. On the other hand, I had made a good faith effort to follow the trail, and sometimes trail decisions that are the most expedient are the best choices. I needed to make a decision.

Then I heard Bob ask, "Wanna just hop on my ATV?" That was the impetus I needed. I gladly accepted and off we went on a very bumpy ride. I hung on as best I could. We rode as far as the ATV was able to go. Bob let me off and then repeated the instructions. I headed into the woods in the direction he was pointing. Sure enough, I popped out on the trail exactly where he said I would. I was lucky to meet Bob.

I made it to Shawnee State Forest. I've been hiking fairly steadily southwest since the Whipple Section. I'm on a part of the Buckeye Trail that takes a dip south and enters Shawnee State Forest. Shawnee State Forest is the largest of the 20 state forests in Ohio and was named for its former inhabitants, the Shawnee Indians. Its nickname is "Little Smokies of Ohio." Going south means more hills, hence its nickname.

Parts of the Buckeye Trail follow the Shawnee Backpack Loop Trail and the Shawnee Wilderness Trail. Any trail in this forest can be described in two words: up-down. The ups are a steep 300′ climb in some places. The gentler climbs are only about 150′. Water is scarce along the trail. At lower elevation the trail is quite overgrown with weeds—knee high to waist high for the entire stretch. All in all, it is a rigorous but do-able hike.

Twenty miles is a good day. At this rate, I figure that I'll be walking into Dayton on June 15, just 11 more days.

Mom and Jim picked me up at 7:00 p.m. We had dinner at the dairy bar in Friendship. We followed up dinner with some ice cream. This is our last night in the cabin. Tomorrow, they go back to Dayton, and I continue my journey.

June 4: Day 77
A Bloody Handprint

I hiked 20 miles to Quinn Chapel.

The entire hike today was on back roads. The weather was hot as usual with a temperature of 90° and a "feels like" temperature near 100°.

I said goodbye to Mom and Jim. They really helped me out the last three days. They provided the cabin for three nights, slackpacked me, fed me, and cheered me on. My mom has always been supportive of my adventures. I appreciate that she encouraged all of her kids to excel wherever their interests lay. I'm happy that she and Jim drove out to see firsthand how I am doing. I think my mom has a deeper appreciation for how physically and mentally demanding this hike is. She looked a bit worried these past few days when she dropped me off at remote places and watched me disappear into the woods.

Maybe her concern was warranted. It has crossed my mind more than once how remote the Buckeye Trail can be in places. Unlike the Appalachian Trail where a hiker who gets hurt just sits down and, within a day, at least ten other hikers pass by. A hiker in the wilderness on the Buckeye Trail will be lying there until deer hunters come by in the fall.

But no worries today. The hike was uneventful. The trail was well marked. No confusing turns and ample blazes. I even had time to take a two-hour siesta in the shade in a cemetery on Abner Hollow Road. Cemeteries make great respites. The grass is usually mowed and soft. The residents are quiet. Rarely are there visitors. Tonight I plan to camp in the cemetery at Quinn Chapel.

Just one more hot climb to the top of the ridge out of the Ohio Brush Creek valley, and I'll call it a day.

Little Smokies of Ohio

On Gift Ridge Road, I passed by the Counterfeit House. This run-down, unassuming single-story building is rich with historical intrigue. The house was built in 1840 by Oliver Tompkins for the purpose of counterfeiting. For $10, a less-than-honest citizen could purchase an authentic-looking $500 dollar bill. The operation was cleverly run. As the story goes, Tompkins would hang a lantern in a small gable window that could be seen by steamboats on the Ohio River two miles away to signal when counterfeit money was available for sale. Today, locals say it's haunted by the Pinkerton agent who was killed in the house trying to uncover the operation. The outline of a bloody handprint can still be seen on the wall or so they say.

I've reached the southern-most point of the Buckeye Trail at the intersection of Waggoner Riffle Road and Abner Hollow Road. It's another milestone. Now I can hike north and west home. I've passed the 1,200 mile mark on this journey.

BUCKEYE
EST. 1959
TRAIL

CHAPTER 11
The Journey Home

June 5: Day 78
From Thru-Hiker to Board Member

I hiked 22 miles to the town of Russellville. The route today was all on back roads.

I awoke in the cemetery at Quinn Chapel to another warm day. High winds and lightning roused me from my tent last night. I staked down my rain fly, but it never did rain.

The day was clear, so I sat outside in the shade of the outhouse to enjoy my morning ritual—two cups of Starbucks instant coffee. I hit the trail around 9:00 a.m. I wish I were an early riser to take advantage of the cool temperatures in the morning.

The hike today was uneventful and pleasant. The miles rolled by easily. I am noticing a change in the topography. The hills are getting smaller and the terrain flatter. There are ups and downs but no steep climbs.

I'm also seeing more farms. Unfortunately, more farms mean poorer stream water quality. Rain washes animal feces, fertilizers, and pesticides into the streams. I haven't seen a stream in a couple of days that looked like a clean source of water.

I'm thirsty, too. On a hot day like today, I can chug down a liter and a half of water at one time and up to eight liters of water a day.

Mom and Jim had stashed some water for me at Quinn Chapel, but that was soon gone. A working soda machine in front of an abandoned grocery store and the kindness of a passing motorist who offered me change, gave me a refreshing Mountain Dew. A few miles later, I was able to hydrate and refill at an outside faucet at a house on Suck Run Road. I had a feeling it would be OK with the owners had they been home.

At mile 15, about eight miles outside of Russellville, I decided to take a short break. As I sat by the side of the road, a truck pulled up. I'm getting used to motorists trying to help me. But when I stood up, I was surprised to see Steve Miller and his daughter, Becky. They were looking for me.

Steve is the computer service coordinator for the Buckeye Trail Association, the section supervisor for the West Union section where I'm currently hiking, and a trustee on the Buckeye Trail Association's board. They were there to help me slackpack the rest of the day and then take me to their home for the night.

Steve and Becky were waiting for me in the park in Russellville when I arrived two hours later. We went to their home in Bethel. Steve's wife, Susan, had dinner waiting for us. They had news to share.

I've been nominated for a Buckeye Trail Association board position. I'm thrilled! How far I have come on such a short journey! When I started this hike, I had been a Buckeye Trail Association member for 11 years, and yet, only had casually hiked the trail. Now, I'm just a few days away from completing the entire trail; I'm a trail maintainer and the new section supervisor of the Troy section. And also nominated as a trustee? I'm not sure how that was even possible since there were no vacant seats on the board. Steve explained that a sitting trustee had voluntarily resigned to make an opening. I'm committed to supporting the Buckeye Trail. Steve and I talked the evening away with ideas on ways to improve and promote the Buckeye Trail. He is a wealth of information on the trail.

I feel like I'm on a hero's journey—the kind in books and movies where the protagonist overcomes multiple challenges and discovers a sense of purpose along the way. I do feel that something wonderful has happened here . . . to me.

June 6: Day 79
My World, My Home, My Job

I hiked 23 miles to Grant Lake. It was another hot, sunny day of road hiking.

I started in Russellville today. Russellville is a country town of about 550 people. It is also home to Seth Blevins, a soldier who was killed in Afghanistan on May 23, 2011. PFC Blevins was in the United States Army Infantry when his Humvee was struck by an improvised explosive device. He and three other soldiers in the vehicle were killed. Seth Blevins had only been in Afghanistan for a month. What a tragic loss. The town is grieving. Banners, signs, and ribbons commemorating Seth's memory are in the park, shop windows, the school, the church—everywhere. The entire town is a monument to the esteem and pride residents have for this young man. He is well loved. I felt their loss.

It was a sobering reminder to me that there's a war going on. Soldiers are putting their lives on the line every day so that I can live well, peaceably, and unafraid. Seth died to protect the lifestyle I sometimes take for granted.

Seth died defending my right to live freely. It's been easy to forget there's another world off the trail that has nothing to do with hiking or the Buckeye Trail.

These past 78 days, the trail has become my world, my home, my job. I have adjusted, adapted, and thrived in this new environment, but I've also been detached from the rest of the world. Maria called on May 2 to tell me that Al Qaeda leader and mastermind of the 9/11 attack that killed 3,000 Americans, Osama bin Laden, was killed by United States Special Forces in Afghanistan. Back home, I would've been trolling news sources for every detail of such an epic event.

It's different on the trail. Solitude is the nature of long-distance, solo hiking. No TV, no radio. I occasionally read the headlines on my smartphone. On the Appalachian Trail, hikers have an old-fashioned form of communication. News travels from hiker to hiker via word-of-mouth. Another hiker approaching from the opposite direction presents an opportunity to exchange information. It's usually trail news—trail conditions, sources of water, animal activity, shelter activity, injury reports and weather forecasts. On the Buckeye Trail, outside news is more accessible, but I'm choosing to concentrate on the hike. I hope Seth's family is doing OK. He's a hero in my book.

I've hiked out of the hills of Appalachia. I can tell because the miles are coming easily which means the terrain is now flat. I'm also noticing that the standard of living has improved. I am no longer walking down windy, gravel roads where people live in hastily built shacks or run-down trailers and where an assortment of discarded, rusty, or broken items litter the yard. The roads are paved, straight, and the homes are nice and well kept. I'm glad to be getting closer to Cincinnati.

I took a break from the heat at a Mennonite church. I drank a half gallon of water from the outside faucet, and lay down on a church pew to rest. I never did see the church caretaker.

I'm spending a second night with the Millers. They were waiting for me when I arrived at the Grant Lake Wildlife Area about 5:30 p.m. I appreciate their support.

I am at the end of another section. What a good feeling! I have nine more days of hiking, 185 miles and three more maps. Wilbur and Orville, are you guys looking forward to seeing me again?

June 7: Day 80
More Is Moron

I hiked 20 miles to East Fork State Park.

The road walking today was uneventful. Half of the route was on roads and the other half was on trails in East Fork State Park. The temperature reached 90 degrees, as predicted. The road surface was so hot in places that the tar bubbled up. A few weeks ago my feet were wet and muddy all day long. Now, the heat and the last 70 miles of road walking have kept them hot and dry. That was about to change.

I've never hiked in East Fork State Park, but I heard the trail was muddy, hilly, and hard hiking. It was. It was also weedy and hard to follow at times. At one point, I was lost. I came out to a large, irregular shaped farm field (just past point 11) and could not find where the trail re-entered the woods. I called off the scavenger hunt after about 45 minutes. I never did find the blaze. I backtracked to the nearest road and walked around. With the heat and my reluctance to wander into the woods in hopes of finding the trail, it was a good decision.

In East Fork State Park, the Buckeye Trail follows part of the Steve Newman "Worldwalker" Perimeter Trail. Steve Newman grew up in the nearby town of Bethel and is the only American to hike solo around the world. Ohio designated this section of trail in his honor. What's unique about the Perimeter Trail is that it not only shares the route with the Buckeye Trail, but also with the American Discovery Trail and the North Country Trail. How many people can say they hiked 20 miles on four long-distance trails today?

For the first time on this hike, I saw another backpacker! I'm not totally surprised. East Fork is a popular backpack trail because of its shorter distances between campsites and good facilities. However, I could see right away that this gal, who was sitting in the weeds in the shade, was a novice backpacker. She had a military-style backpack which looked like it weighed 60 pounds, and a pit bull, which was not on a leash. Two, full one-gallon jugs of water sat next to her in the weeds, and a semi-automatic hand gun lay on top of her backpack. She looked beat up from the heat and in no hurry to move. Our conversation was short. The only information she offered was that she was hiking the Perimeter Trail. I kept moving and left her to rest.

Two common expressions describe an over-packed backpacker: "Less on is good; more on is moron" and the gentler, "the sum total weight of your backpack represents your fears." From our 30-second encounter, I could tell her fears were guiding what she thought she needed to bring on the trail. She knew it was going to be hot, so she brought plenty of water. She knew she would be hiking and camping out alone in the woods, so she brought her dog and a gun. She was probably carrying a lot of items she didn't need or wouldn't use. I've seen backpackers carry cans of food, pots, pans, cooking utensils and a tent that sleeps a family of five. It's a common mistake among inexperienced hikers. Packing efficiently is a skill that takes time to develop.

My long day came to a close when I emerged at a road to a boat ramp at 8:00 p.m. I had hoped to camp in East Fork tonight, but I didn't make the miles I had wanted. Besides, the humidity was suffocating. I gladly accepted Steve's offer to stay over another night.

June 8: Day 81
I Take Heat Seriously

I hiked 20 miles to Batavia, 12 miles in East Fork State Park and the last eight on roads. Temperatures reached 95°.

I said goodbye to Steve, Susan, and Becky Miller today. They made a stranger-turned-friend feel very welcomed in their home.

The trail in East Fork was a pleasant walk. The trail was well blazed. The shade of the trees cooled the heat a few degrees. The ups and downs of the horse trail were mostly graded which made for easier hiking. The trail was dry, but it was still rough. I don't know which is harder—walking in wet, mucky hoof depressions or in dry, choppy ones.

The trail in East Fork State Park went by two picnic areas. I was hoping to refill my water bottles, but the water faucets were not working at either picnic area. I saw a half-empty water bottle on a picnic table that someone had left behind. I decided to drink the rest of it. It was warm, but it tasted fine. Having enough water is extremely important in this hot weather. Without water, my hike would shut down in a matter of hours.

I take heat very seriously. On an Appalachian Trail hike in July of 1998 in New York, the heat and humidity was brutal, much like this weather has been, and I was sweating profusely, much like I have been these past weeks. Heat exhaustion takes time to develop; so when I was feeling overheated and fatigued that day, it seemed normal on such a hot day. Feeling like I was dehydrated, I began guzzling water.

Then something went terribly wrong. I suddenly became nauseous and collapsed. I lay in the dirt not far from where I had vomited, unable to move. I remember feeling swarms of mosquitoes attacking like dive bombers around my head and thinking I should swat them away, but I was too weak to even lift my arm. I don't know how long I lay there before I managed to crawl into the shade by a stream. I lay by the stream for several hours. When my body finally cooled down somewhat, I walked two miles into town, but I was still dizzy and disoriented. It took two days of rest in an air-conditioned room to recover, both physically and mentally.

Turns out, I wasn't dehydrated. I had hyponatremia, also known as water intoxication. It's from drinking *too* much water. The water

Backpack trail, East Fork State Park

flushed essential nutrients like sodium and potassium out of my body. Drinking too much water without proper electrolyte replacement had poisoned me. It was a traumatic experience and a lesson well learned.

I lay down in the shade to take a short siesta to avoid getting overheated. For the past several weeks, an afternoon nap has become part of my daily hiking routine.

I'm getting close to home territory and familiar faces. My friend Jenny Waters lives in Batavia and offered to host me for a night. Jenny is a member of my hiking group, Dayton Hikers. I took her on her first backpacking trip three years ago.

June 9: Day 82
Boy, It Feels Good!

I hiked 25 miles to Eden Park in Cincinnati with temperatures near 90°. The route was on roads, bike paths, and sidewalks. The day started out as a rural hike and ended as an urban hike.

Jenny dropped me off at the United Dairy Farmers in Batavia at 7:30 a.m. I drank a coffee and had a light breakfast before setting out. The

10-mile walk to Milford was scenic and quiet. It is the last of southern rural Ohio that I will see on this journey.

I arrived at the outskirts of Milford about 10:00 a.m. and soon reached the "Trails Junction" at Milford where eight, long-distance trails intersect and then stretch across the United States in all four cardinal directions. These biking, hiking, and paddling trails total over 22,000 miles. I stood in front of the ten-foot wooden sign which pointed trail directions and thought about all of the adventure possibilities. If I go left, I follow the American Discovery Trail out to Eden Park in Cincinnati and eventually onto the west coast or south on the Underground Railroad route to the Gulf of Mexico.

If I go back the way I came and stay on the Sea-to-Sea Long Distance Trail, I'd be in Maine. If I turn right, I follow the Buckeye Trail, the Little Miami Scenic Trail, the Little Miami River Water Trail, the Ohio to Erie Trail, and the North Country Trail, the latter which heads straight north to Michigan and onto North Dakota.

Which way to go? At the Junction, the Buckeye Trail splits in two directions. The main circuit north travels up the bike path along the

Southern terminus of the Buckeye Trail, Cincinnati

Little Miami River towards Dayton. The southern route is a 13-mile spur trail to Eden Park, the Buckeye Trail southern terminus. I turned south.

The last miles to Eden Park were sidewalk. For the first time in weeks, the Buckeye Trail was full of people—walkers, joggers, skate boarders, roller bladders, and for the first time in weeks, I once again looked out of place in an urban environment. Backpack or no back-pack, I cruised happily down the sidewalk knowing I had friends and family who have been cheering me on throughout this journey waiting at Eden Park to greet me.

As I approached, seeing the Ohio River overwhelmed me with emotion. I had forgotten how beautiful the river valley looks from the

Eden Park, Cincinnati

bluff and how proud I am to be an Ohioan. My friend, Christine Plepys, my cousins, Bob and Brenda Schwieterman, and I enjoyed a small celebration of food and drink at the park. Their welcome back marks the final stage of this journey.

I've now come 1,325 miles on this journey. I've turned the last of the four corners of Ohio. That means I'm done hiking south, east, and west and every direction in between. I've run the gauntlet of the Buckeye Trail in southern Ohio and survived. Tomorrow, I'll head north for the final 115 miles to Dayton. I'm in home territory and, boy, it feels good.

June 10: Day 83
Signs of Summer

I hiked about 14 miles north on the Little Miami River.

I spent last night with Bob and Brenda in West Chester. I showered, did laundry, and had a delicious dinner. When I looked in the mirror, I noticed that my shoulders are wider than my belly. No, my shoulders did not get larger on this hike. I've lost 15 pounds. Hiking the entire Buckeye Trail has been a great diet and exercise plan. I wish I could retain my great physical shape after this hike. It will be hard to do when I return to life in suburbia.

I didn't hit the trail until 2:00 p.m. I piddled around this morning doing gear chores—cleaning, sorting, pitching, organizing. Chores are a fact of life even for a backpacker. My cousin Bob dropped me off in Milford around 12:30 p.m., but I could see rain coming on the horizon and headed for the shelter of a coffee shop. Sure enough, it poured for a good hour and a half.

I started my trek north on the Little Miami River bike path at the Junction after the storm passed. The cool rain water on the hot asphalt created a steamy mist that refracted the sunlight. It made the bike path shimmer.

I passed another backpacker, I think. A young, attractive lady in a bikini top and shorts with long flowing hair was heading south. She carried a wooden hiking stick, a small knapsack for a pack and had a bongo drum slung over her shoulder. She looked to be headed somewhere fun. We exchanged "hellos." I thought briefly about turning around and hiking with her, but I'm homeward bound.

Loveland was bubbling with activity when I arrived around 5:00 p.m. It was a warm Friday evening, and everyone was outside enjoying the weather. The ice cream shops and sidewalk cafes were crowded. People were out walking, riding bikes, and having picnics in the park. I sat on a bench, drank a Mountain Dew, and soaked in these signs of summer.

The idyllic outdoor scene came to a quick end when a severe thunderstorm rolled in. Lightning filled the sky and large booms of thunder chased people indoors. A hard rain pelted the ground. In a matter of minutes, everyone was gone except for a couple of cyclists taking cover in a picnic shelter and me.

I waited awhile and then resumed hiking in the rain. Around 8:00 p.m., the rain quit, and the sun tried to come out. It never did emerge, but it gave the western sky an eerie, beautiful orange glow. Water dripped from the trees as if it were still raining. I took a deep breath and inhaled the freshness in the air.

Just when I was gaining on lost miles from today's rain, I happened across the perfect camping spot. It had a picnic table covered by a roof and a gravel pad for parking bicycles. I decided to call it a day and made myself at home. I set up my tent on the gravel pad and strung a line above the picnic table to hang my wet clothes. A few cyclists peddled by. Daylight faded as I climbed into my tent.

June 11: Day 84
A Feeling of Sadness

I hiked 30 miles to Caesar Creek State Park. I am on map 26 of 26! Only 74 miles to go.

I awoke to rain this morning. A late-night storm had brought a steady rain. I made breakfast and coffee with my camp stove at the picnic table under the shelter and watched the wet bikers, joggers, and walkers go by on the bike path. I was going to be right there with them . . . as soon as the rain stopped.

I'm proud to say that I've become a hiking machine. What a change from just a few weeks ago! My body has finally adapted to the daily routine of carrying a backpack dozens of miles on hard surfaces. My feet don't hurt; my leg muscles have hardened. I have lost pounds of body weight. My skin is getting tan, and my beard is growing. I can stroll up to an unfamiliar woods at sunset, find a place to camp, and get a good night of sleep. I can wake up the next day and do it all over again.

Months on the trail have been transforming. Hiking has always been my personal fountain of youth. I've become mentally and physically tough from hours of strenuous activity in an outdoor environment. I feel young because my body is strong. I also gain a youthful mental vitality. I'm adaptive, free, fearless, and confident in my skills to manage unknowns. I'm thriving.

I popped in my ear buds and scrolled down my play list to the loud, fast-paced, pop rock music of the B52s. I put my boots on cruise control. As I neared Kings Island, I could hear the sounds of screaming people having fun on the roller coasters. I passed the former Kings Powder Mill where explosives for the Spanish-American War were made. I zipped by Fort Ancient, a former ceremonial site of the Hopewell Indians, Morgan's Canoe Livery, and crossed under I-71.

Two miles before Oregonia, I was greeted by familiar faces. Brent and Amy Anslinger and their two young daughters came out on bikes to find me. Brent and Amy thru-hiked the Buckeye Trail in 2003. As I walked to Oregonia, the Anslingers rode alongside. We had supper in

Campsite along the Little Miami River bike path

Oregonia, and then my friends slackpacked me to my day's destination—the Day Use Lodge at Caesar Creek State Park. When I arrived at the lodge a few hours later, Brent and Amy were waiting for me with adult beverages and brownies. It was wonderful having their company and their support.

I can't believe I'm at Caesar Creek State Park. I have hiked on the trails here dozens of times and enjoyed many outings at the day lodge. This is the first time I've ever camped on its back porch under the stars. That means one thing. I'm almost home, and I'm also almost finished with this journey.

The thought of being almost finished brought a sudden feeling of sadness. I'm almost done hiking the longest thru-hike I've ever done in terms of miles and time. I'm almost done walking the circumference of my home state, through its five ecoregions each with its own unique climate, geology, plant and animal life. I'm almost done with the most unique and incredibly rewarding hiking experience I've ever had.

I have to admit that I relished slipping out of my role as an ordinary suburbanite every day to be a Buckeye Trail thru-hiker, an outdoor adventurer, an ordinary person who was doing something extraordinary. I'm going to miss waking up in the morning with an eagerness to lay down miles and embrace whatever unknowns the day holds. I'm going to miss this hike.

June 12: Day 85
I Have a Certain Identity

I hiked 24 miles just south of Xenia. The weather was a pleasant 70° with a light breeze.

I was tired from hiking 30 miles yesterday and didn't rouse until well after sunrise. I packed up my tent at the Caesar Creek State Park day lodge and headed into the woods and down the trail. History has it that a slave named Caesar, whose master had been killed during a Shawnee Indian raid, was taken captive and adopted by the Indians. Caesar, it is claimed, was so fond of fishing in the stream near here that he named it after himself.

The dam at Caesar Creek was built in the 1970s. I can recall visiting the area as a boy before the lake was built. My buddies and I used to hang out on the beach during my college days. The marina is busy today. I passed a line of boats each waiting to put in the lake at the boat ramp.

My mind started to drift back to yesterday's thoughts. The trail has been my home for the past 85 days. It's my safe place. I'm dreading the inevitable post-hike adjustment. Every long-distance hiker goes through it. It's the bittersweet, conflicted feeling of being anxious to be home, but not anxious, of being happy to be finished, but not happy. The hiking skills that I've perfected—wilderness navigation, stream crossing, fire building, backcountry conservation—aren't much use back home in suburbia. On the trail when people see a guy with a beard and a backpack, they think, "Oh, there's a hiker!" When seeing a bearded guy with a pack walking the streets of Dayton, people think, "Oh, there's a homeless person." It's the difference between being admired and being pitied, of being looked up to and being looked down on. I embrace life on the trail. How am I going to retain the vibrancy I feel?

On the trail, I have a certain identity, a mission, a defined purpose. People I meet along the way, most strangers to me, reinforce my sense of purpose. Early on, when I had only hiked a few hundred miles and told people about my 1,444-mile journey around Ohio, they were in awe, often in a state of jaw-dropping disbelief. They said it was wonderful that I am tackling such a long journey. I felt so good whenever I'd hear it. It boosted my confidence and my commitment to continue.

Lately, though, the closer I get to home I've noticed a change in reactions when I tell people I am hiking the Buckeye Trail. Now when I say I've hiked over 1,200 or 1,300 miles since March 20 and have only a few hundred to go, they don't seem to know how to respond. They usually say something like, "Gee, you've been out a long time," like they're not especially impressed.

Is there less empathy because I've mastered the hardest part of the trail? Or perhaps being in my shoes at this point doesn't seem like that much of a challenge? For whatever reason, it feels disappointing that encouragement from strangers has stopped. It makes me feel as if I've lost something of what made me feel so special.

Maybe I was so low today because the hiking on these mucky horse trails in Caesar's Creek for ten miles has been so miserable.

I eventually left Caesar Creek State Park and hiked on roads to Spring Valley and back to the Little Miami River bike path. I called it a day just before reaching Xenia. I am spending the night with my mother and Jim who live in the south Dayton area.

June 13: Day 86
The Journey Makes the Person

I hiked 25 miles to Springfield. The route was mostly on the Little Miami River bike path except for some road walking in Springfield. Perfect hiking weather: sunny, breezy, and 75°.

I stopped in Xenia for a break. I got a cup of coffee and three Krispy Kreme donuts. It was not a healthy snack, but it sure tasted good. My body is craving calories. With hiker's appetite, *what* a hiker consumes is less important than *how much* he or she consumes. There were times, especially in southern Ohio, when I pulled the highest-calorie Little Debbie cakes I could find off the grocery shelf. It was fast fuel. Unfortunately, it'll take weeks for my hiker's appetite to wear off. I hope I can fight the urge to overeat so I can keep the lost pounds off. I guess it'll be another adjustment to life in suburbia. I'm so comfortable in my life on the trail that returning home feels harder than leaving.

I stopped for a late lunch in Yellow Springs. Founded in 1825, this little village has turned its historic buildings into boutiques, bookstores, coffee shops, restaurants, and art galleries. The Chamber of Commerce describes it this way: "The community is culturally diverse, values self-expression and prides itself on being open, friendly and creative."

Those of us from the area like it because of its "hippie town" feel. In Yellow Springs, everybody fits in, even a bearded hiker.

From Yellow Springs, the trail heads north for ten miles to downtown Springfield, then turns back south to Fairborn in a U-shaped pattern. It is literally a hairpin turn. This route doesn't make sense to a hiker who is going from Cincinnati to Dayton. It shouldn't be part of the trail. Anyway, tomorrow I'll leave Springfield and start the last 25-mile stretch. It is time to end this hike.

I'm going to end this entry with my favorite quote: "Does the person make the journey, or does the journey make the person?"

When I "make the journey," I focus on the planning, the logistics, the sights, and the activities. That's what I call the outer journey. What I forgot about was the inner journey—the part of the journey that "makes the person." Over the last weeks, I have transitioned from the outer journey to the inner journey. The inner journey is personal growth. The inner journey pushed me to change, to adapt, and to adjust to the demands I encountered.

Any long-distance trail is "the great equalizer." The snakes, ticks, and mosquitoes don't care who you are. The rain or the wind isn't going to stop because you're uncomfortable. You get no sympathy from Mother Nature because you're having a bad day. When your poles or your boots give out, you figure out how to fix or replace them. When your feet ache from miles of road walking, you change socks, patch up the blisters, and march on. When you've lost the trail, you put your navigation skills to the test. When the going is so rough that you feel like quitting, you keep going. When the wind is so strong that it lifts you off your feet, you persevere. The more hardships you endure, the more you grow in mental toughness, the more rewarding the journey becomes. The outer journey is less important to me. I am a firm believer that the journey makes the person. This journey has made me—stronger, more confident, better.

June 14: Day 87
The Freedom of the Simple Life

I hiked 16 miles from Springfield to Fairborn. I am now a mere nine miles from finishing this hike!

The hike today was all on roads except for a very short stretch of trail in Cold Springs Park in Fairborn. I hiked fast today. I felt like "a horse heading for the barn."

I am anxiously ready for my last day of hiking. I am ready to be at Deeds Point to see Wilbur and Orville, where I started my hike on March 20.

The impact of what I've nearly accomplished is starting to sink in. I'm feeling happy. I'm feeling excited. I'm feeling grateful. Maria is driving in tonight from Cleveland to finish the hike with me. We haven't seen each other since my birthday on May 15. Our relationship is blossoming. It'll be a sweet reunion.

My friends at Five Rivers MetroParks are planning a celebration for tomorrow. Brent Anslinger sent me a link to a news release that ran in today's edition of the *Dayton Most Metro* announcing my arrival to Deeds Point tomorrow. A news reporter and a camera crew will be there for an interview. Members of my Dayton Hiker's group are meeting me on the trail three miles from Deeds Point at Eastwood MetroPark to walk in with me. I'm getting superstar treatment.

Tomorrow's final hike will be a joyous event. So, today is my final day of solo hiking. This is the last day I'll have the trail all to myself. I'm savoring this last bit of freedom the simple life provides. I've learned so much about myself on this journey. I've learned that I could stay on trail for a three-month stretch and cover over 1,444 miles. I've learned that I have a lot more perseverance in me than I ever imagined. I've learned the limitations of my physical and mental capabilities. I've learned that I could have a wonderful hiking experience hiking in Ohio. Nowhere on the Appalachian Trail have I ever experienced the hospitality and generosity from strangers than I have experienced on the Buckeye Trail. I've learned to appreciate the smallest kindnesses—a piece of chocolate, hot meals, sandwiches, soda, money for a soda, offers of money for whatever, bottles of water, invitations to rest or sleep under a covered porch, in a horse stable, or in a barn, shuttle rides, and offers of lodging from complete strangers. I've learned to appreciate a warm breeze on a warm day, the shade of a tree, a day with rain, a day without rain, and the sunrise on a frosty morning. I have come to love the Buckeye Trail.

June 15: Day 88
Once You Achieve, You Have a Duty to Inspire

I hiked the remaining nine miles of the Buckeye Trail into Dayton to Deeds Point. More obstacles were to come.

The final leg of my journey began on the bike path in Fairborn at Colonel Glenn Highway and Kauffman Road. The Troy Section of the Buckeye Trail starts here. I'm so happy that Maria is with me.

The day was overcast. Rain was in the forecast. It seems appropriate since I have hiked so many miles of this hike in the rain. Today the rain is just liquid sunshine.

We reached the Wright Brothers Memorial Park after about four miles of easy walking. The park sits on the northern edge of Wright Patterson Air Force Base and at the top of a bluff which overlooks the Huffman Dam and the former flying field of the Wright Brothers. We had time for a tour of the Huffman Prairie Flying Field Interpretive Center. I haven't been here since I was a little boy. The exhibits in this center highlight the activities and accomplishments of the Wright Brothers after they made their first flight in 1903 at Kitty Hawk in North Carolina. The Wright Flyer III, considered world's first practical aircraft, was invented and flown here in Dayton. The genius of the Wright brothers brought aviation to humankind.

It started to rain. Maria and I donned rain gear before hopping back on the trail. I had an interview appointment with Chris Rizer, a reporter for the *Dayton Daily News* at Eastwood MetroPark about two miles away. We followed the blue blazes from Memorial Park into the woods, and then they disappeared. I knew the direction we were supposed to go, but without a defined route, we had to forge our way. It was quite the process. We followed the bike path, then ran across four-lanes of SR-444, walked along active railroad tracks and climbed down the railroad trestle at Springfield Street. We found the blue blazes again on the other side of the train tracks and headed towards Eastwood MetroPark.

With only three-and-a-half miles to go of this 1,444-mile journey, about an hour's walk and just when I could almost see the skyline of downtown Dayton, one last adventure was about to unfold. Before I explain what happened, let me back up a little. I've been living in two worlds since I started this hike back in March—the hiking world and the non-hiking. I knew from the beginning of this hike that the Buckeye Trail was not going to be a wilderness experience. A wilderness experience has lots of overlap with the other hikers, an established hiking community, a trail culture, and of course, lots and lots of forest. The Buckeye Trail experience has more overlap with the non-hiking world—cities, towns, villages, pavement walking, restaurants, convenience stores, lots of people who aren't hikers, and few forests. I was feeling very confident that I had mastered the skill of hiking in both worlds. My skills were about to be tested.

To get to Eastwood MetroPark from Springfield Street, the Buckeye Trail goes a short distance on water well fields owned by the City of

Dayton. When we arrived at the well fields, I knew the Buckeye Trail traversed well field land. The blazes are painted there; the map shows that the trail goes through here. However, as we began to cross, two City of Dayton Water Department employees pulled up in a truck and blocked our path.

"What are you doing?" the driver asked.

"I'm hiking the Buckeye Trail. The Buckeye Trail comes through here, and I'm finishing my Buckeye Trail thru-hike," I replied politely.

"No, you're not. No trespassing on this property. This is the Dayton Well Field," the driver replied rather impolitely.

"Well, the Buckeye Trail comes through here. Here's the map to prove it. See?"

The look on his face told me the answer to that question was no. He didn't want to look at the map. Not once in the last 88 days did anyone try to stop my hike—not law enforcement, not a land owner, and especially not a city worker. I didn't dare let my irritation show in my voice.

"Do you see these blue blazes on the poles?" I asked. "That means the Buckeye Trail comes through here."

"No, it doesn't. Absolutely no trespassing. I can't let you by." He was firm in his resolve.

"Well, I'm *really* certain the Buckeye Trail goes through here, and I'm *really* certain I'm allowed to be here. This is the last day of my 1,444-mile hike, and in about a half mile, I'm meeting up with a news reporter who's doing a *Dayton Daily News* article about my hike."

"Nope. You cannot pass," he insisted. He wasn't impressed with the fact that I had walked the entire state of Ohio or that he was in the presence of a hometown celebrity about to enjoy his "15 minutes of fame" in the media spotlight. I also surmised he had no understanding of the significance of completing a long-distance hike.

Reasoning with him was going nowhere. "Would you please call your supervisor?" I hoped he wouldn't object to my request to go over his head.

"I'll call my supervisor, but it's not going to do any good," he grunted.

He got out his phone, looking at me out of the corner of his eye as he dialed. I guess he wanted to watch us in case Maria and I tried to make a run for it.

"Hey, Charlie, there's some guy walking through our property who says he's hiking the Buckeye Trail. I'm telling him he's not allowed to come through here, but he insisted I call you."

Then I heard, "Yeah (pause). Yeah (pause). Oh! (pause). Oh! (pause). OK. Bye."

He turned to me and begrudgingly conceded, "Yeah, you're right. You're allowed to come through here." He backed his truck up and pulled out of our way.

"Thank you!" I called out cheerily, happy to have diplomatically resolved this unexpected dilemma of the hiker in a non-hiker world.

The reporter from the *Dayton Daily News* was at Eastwood MetroPark as planned. We talked for about an hour. The article will appear in the Sunday (June 19) edition of the *Dayton Daily News* in the "Life" section. I also did a short interview with a videographer from the local FOX45/ABC22 TV station in town. Maybe I'll be on the evening news!

Around 2:30 p.m., members of the Dayton Hikers group starting arriving to hike the last three miles with me from Eastwood MetroPark to Deeds Point. It was a great turnout! I was gratified to see my friend Scallion among the crowd. Together with my friends, we walked the last three miles of the Buckeye Trail along the Mad River bike path to downtown Dayton. I was filled with emotion as we walked along a river I have known my entire life. Today, it's different; I'm different.

As we approached Deeds Point, I could see the fountains along the river shooting water into the sky. I saw the Dayton skyline and Deeds Point for the first time in three months. A crowd of about 20 people had assembled at Deeds Point to help me celebrate the finish of my hike. They were waving American flags and cheering me on. Someone placed a necklace made of buckeyes around my neck.

The final stretch of the trail to Deeds Point MetroPark goes over a foot bridge over the Mad River. As I crossed the bridge, I got a blast of energy and decided to jump into the air and kick my heels together in jubilation. It was spontaneous and unrehearsed. Lisa Powell, a photographer for the *Dayton Daily News*, caught this moment on camera. It felt so good to finish this hike and be back home!

I gave "high fives" and hugs to the crowd waiting for me at Deeds Point. They continued cheering, chanting "Captain Blue" and waving flags. To close the loop on this circuit hike, I took the final ten more

Heel click at trail finish, downtown Dayton

steps to the statues of Wilbur and Orville Wright. I gave them both a big hug and yelled "Off Trail!" The hike was officially over.

Afterwards, we went to the Outdoor Recreation office of the Five Rivers MetroParks on Saint Clair Street in downtown Dayton. Brent Anslinger and Mike "Scallion" Fanelli had cake, ice cream, and soda pop there for everyone. A slide show of my Buckeye Trail photos was showing on a large screen. I had taken 2,047 pictures. I got a chance to greet everyone and chat with them. Many of these people had faithfully followed my blog every day. Some told me it was part of their daily routine to check my progress, to look at the pictures I posted daily, to read the stories about the people I met and the adventures I was having. They were hiking the Buckeye Trail vicariously through me.

The crowd sang a belated "Happy Birthday" song to me at my mother's request. A short question and answer period about my hike followed. The festivities ended by 5:30 p.m. It was a wonderful homecoming. Now it was time to return to normal life, whatever that may be.

I remember the feeling I had when I finished the Appalachian Trail for the first time in 1998. Climbing Katahdin in Maine is like graduation

Captain Blue

day for an AT hiker. The effort of months of blood, sweat, and tears finally pays off. The excited anticipation of the final climb begins 100 miles away and builds as glimpses of the great mountain come into view from vistas along the trail. I remember the thrill of cresting the summit of Katahdin and seeing the sign on Baxter Peak that marked my final destination, the northern terminus of the Appalachian Trail and the end of my long journey. Reaching Baxter Peak did not feel like the end of anything. I sensed it was the beginning of something great. I went on to hike the Appalachian Trail end-to-end two more times.

I'm feeling the same way now. Yes, this hike ended today. I sense, however, that something great is in store. This journey has changed me. I have a new love in my life who loves me back and is proud of what I've accomplished. I have decided to leave behind the 27 years I've invested into a career in IT and pursue my love of the outdoors. I'm ready to spring into action as a new board member of the BTA and a new section supervisor. Fresh ideas for ways to promote the Buckeye Trail have been percolating in my head for the past weeks. I have a list of recommendations for fellow section supervisors on ways to improve the trail for hikers and places where the trail can be rerouted for safer travel. I want to collect feedback from people who hike the trail and see what their greatest needs are. Most of all, I want to share my adventure on the Buckeye Trail with other people. I fully believe in the unwritten creed of the honorable adventurer: once you achieve, you have a duty to inspire. What the Buckeye Trail needs most is hikers. I want to recruit new members and inspire them with the wonderful adventures that await them on the Buckeye Trail.

See you on the trail.
Andy "Captain Blue" Niekamp

BUCKEYE
EST. 1959
TRAIL

EPILOGUE
Beyond the Hike

It was a Tuesday night in Piqua, a mid-sized town in Ohio's Miami Valley, January 2017. The last of the audience members were making their way out the door. I powered down the laptop and stowed equipment as I answered a few more questions about my 2011 solo thru-hike of the Buckeye Trail. This was the 33rd presentation I have given about my 88-day journey around Ohio since completing it six years ago.

I've given this presentation, or a variation of it, not just in Piqua but in Cadiz, Cincinnati, Columbus, Cleveland, Dayton, Kettering, Lima, Maria Stein, New Bremen, Minister, Piqua, Shawnee, Tipp City, Versailles, Michigan and Kentucky—in short, all over Ohio and beyond. All in all, over 1,000 people have attended my program and heard about my wonderful experiences on the Buckeye Trail.

My trail blog, on which this book is based, reached even more people. Blog records indicate 121,000 visitors. Some of those visitors actually contacted me directly, asking for advice on hiking the Buckeye Trail or just to express that they've been inspired to try long-distance hiking.

Hiking the Buckeye Trail came at a time in my life that I can best summarize as a watershed moment. Many changes have transpired since 2011 that were a related or a direct result of this hike. I've had enough adventures to write another book. I'll save them for another time. For now, I'll try to encapsulate what has transpired over the years since my hike.

I kept my commitment to the Buckeye Trail.

Trustee of the Buckeye Trail Association: I served as a trustee for the Buckeye Trail Association completing my two-year term in 2013.

Troy Section Supervisor: By July 2011, I was full-throttle as Troy section supervisor. My first task was to re-open the section of trail through the Wright Memorial where Maria and I had lost the trail on the final day of my hike. I supported county officials in moving the Buckeye Trail off road and onto newly linked bike pathways in three places. I also lent a hand in sprucing up the trail for the July 2011 North Country Trail Association annual conference in Dayton. We installed 12 new signs. I may be partial, but the Troy Section is one of the best blazed and well-signaged sections on the trail.

Friends of the Buckeye Trail: Also in July 2011, I set up the first ever Buckeye Trail Meetup site called *Friends of the Buckeye Trail*. My vision was to have the site serve as a state-wide social network for Buckeye Trail hikers. Hike leaders from all corners of Ohio were able to organize and post hikes. The success of the Friends of the Buckeye Trail Meetup birthed other Buckeye Trail Meetup groups including the first chapters of the Buckeye Trail Association. Members and non-members can connect, socialize, and hike the trail together.

Buckeye TrailFest: I created and managed the first Buckeye TrailFest. This event transformed the annual meeting, a tradition of 50 years, into a state-wide trail festival. It was held at Fort Ancient in April 2012. Two hundred people attended that first year, which was at the time, the largest ever Buckeye Trail Association gathering. I coined the slogan: "Get Hiking, Get Dirty, Get Involved, Get Connected" as the theme. Buckeye TrailFest was, and still is, a multi-day event in which members from all parts of Ohio gather for hiking, field trips, socializing, and to attend programs and the annual business meeting.

Life Is Better on the Buckeye Trail *Fundraiser:* I raised thousands of dollars for the Buckeye Trail Association from the sale of my *Life Is Better on the Buckeye Trail* shirts. I got the idea for this shirt in Navarre on my thru-hike. Darlene Karoly designed the shirt. I printed the shirts at my expense and donated the entire sales collected to the Buckeye Trail Association. The theme was popular and later imprinted on patches and bumper stickers.

Superstar Award: In 2012, I received the Superstar Award from the Buckeye Trail Association for promoting the Buckeye Trail and pioneering Buckeye TrailFest. The award recognizes superior service over time, an accomplishment I had reached in just ten months.

Elimination of the Springfield Spur: In 2013, I was successful in leading the effort to eliminate the 15-mile up-and-back Springfield spur. It made the connection between the Caesar Creek section and the Troy section more direct by reducing the meander factor.

Buckeye Trail Winter Hike at Caesar Creek: In 2014, I created the first annual winter hike on the Buckeye Trail at Caesar Creek State Park. It is now an event that hikers from all over southwest Ohio look forward to every January. Participants can choose from one of five different guided hikes, ranging from 3 to 13 miles. Afterwards, hikers enjoy a warm potluck meal, a raffle, and plenty of time to network with other hikers.

Buckeye Trail Membership Drive: In 2016, I helped create and manage the first Buckeye Trail membership drive. It was held at a brew pub in Dayton and was wildly successful. Over 149 new members signed up in one night growing overall Buckeye Trail Association membership by 10%. The membership drive featured socializing, food, drink, fast-paced programs, and a raffle. I developed the membership drive format to be copied easily. Since then, eleven membership drives have taken place, and I've been part of many of them. Over 400 new members have been added to the ranks as a result.

Google Trekker Project: Other volunteer projects in the Dayton area in which I've participated have benefited the Buckeye Trail. In 2016, I partnered with Five Rivers MetroParks to lease a Google Street View Trekker backpack to record hundreds of miles of Dayton-area trails and park destinations. This 50-pound backpack, equipped with 15 cameras that snap pictures every two seconds journeyed through 18 MetroParks and 20 regional parks. It was the most comprehensive 360° virtual imagery project of its kind in Ohio capturing over 600 miles of trails. Nearly 100 miles of the Buckeye Trail from Cincinnati to Dayton to Piqua were recorded and are available now online for viewing. Buckeye Trail hikers are able to take a virtual tour of multiple sections of the Buckeye Trail before they set foot on the trail.

Warrior 150 Challenge: In 2017, I assisted in planning and leading a series of hikes, most of which are on the Buckeye Trail, to honor our veterans and to celebrate 150 years of Dayton's VA Medical Center. The Warrior 150 Hiking Challenge was a series of five hikes from March to October. Four of the five hikes were on the Buckeye Trail in the Troy, St. Marys, and Caesar Creek sections. Each was about 25 miles long.

Trail Angels: Fellow Dayton Hikers members and I have become trail angels. We serve on the unpublished list of Buckeye Trail angels. Buckeye Trail hikers who come through the Dayton area can count on our hospitality.

Hiking continues to be my passion.

Ohio To Erie Trail Thru-Hike: In 2013, I took another Ohio trails journey. I wanted to show that the 320-mile Ohio To Erie multi-use trail could be backpacked. Maria and Scallion joined me on parts of that three-week journey. It was another first thru-hike adventure that took me from the river banks of the Ohio in Cincinnati to the shores of Lake Erie in Cleveland.

Other Long Distance Trails: I have completed a fourth end-to-end hike of the entire Appalachian Trail and began my fifth. I also thru-hiked other long-distance trails including: the 485-mile Colorado Trail, the 319-mile Sheltowee Trace in Kentucky, the 280-mile Long Trail in Vermont, the 270-mile Superior Hiking Trail in Minnesota, 180-mile Ozark Highlands Trail in Arkansas, the 110-mile Bartram Trail in Georgia, the 70-mile Foothills Trail in South Carolina, and the short, but tough 30-mile Art Loeb Trail in North Carolina.

Dayton Hikers Meetup Group: I continue to inspire others to go hiking, live a healthier lifestyle, explore nature, and make friends by leading the Dayton Hikers group. Dayton Hikers remains the largest outdoor recreation group in Dayton. We are the most active hiking Meetup group in Ohio. With over 4,000 members, we average over 1,000 events per year. We are making Dayton a better place to live.

Hiking is now my profession.

In 2012, I formed Outdoor Adventure Connection LLC and named myself the Chief Adventure Officer. I became a backpacking instructor as a way to turn my hiking passion into a profession. Hundreds of people have attended my backpacking workshops which range from a one-night outing in a local park to a multi-day trip on the Appalachian Trail. Through Outdoor Adventure Connection, many have gained the skills and confidence to go on their own backpacking trips including long-distance hikes. I became a Leave No Trace a Master Educator, and a Wilderness First Responder.

Where to from here?

I don't know for sure. But it will involve hiking, hikers, and trails. I have never done a hike before or since my Buckeye Trail hike that has held such long-lasting significance. The commitment I made to give back as a volunteer, to inspire others to hike, to help others to embrace the wonder of the outdoors is still as vibrant as the day I stepped off the Buckeye Trail. One thing hasn't changed as a result of my epic hike. I'm still Captain Blue, in search of the next new adventure. That will never change. I'll always be Captain Blue on the move.

HIKING THE BUCKEYE TRAIL

The Buckeye Trail Association

Are you interested in hiking the Buckeye Trail? Whether your interest lies in hiking short sections or doing the entire trail in one journey, the Buckeye Trail Association is for you. Here are the benefits to becoming a member of the Buckeye Trail Association.

Hike with like-minded people. Organized hikes, offered all-year round, are plentiful. Hosted by local BTA chapters and other BTA groups, experienced hike leaders set up the hike location, distance, and other logistics. Whether it's the annual winter hike or monthly circuit hikes, organizers find fun and creative ways to get people on the trail.

Get even more personal and join one or more of the five local chapters located around the state. You'll have an instant trail family! Local chapters also organize off-trail activities, like presentations and gatherings. You can choose from hundreds of chapter events.

Get connected. The highlight of the year is the annual Buckeye TrailFest, Ohio's premiere trail festival. Buckeye TrailFest is the largest gathering of BT hikers, members, volunteers and enthusiasts of the year. It includes the annual meeting of the BTA as well as many educational workshops, outings on the BT in the local region, evening entertainment, and best of all, time to enjoy the company of others who are interested and passionate about the BT. Also included in membership are quarterly issues of the *Trailblazer.* This BTA-published newsletter keeps the BT community up-to-date on issues affecting the trail and its members with articles, pictures, and trail news.

Get involved. The Buckeye Trail Association is always looking for volunteers to be trail stewards—Section Supervisor, Trail Maintainer, Trail Adopter, or a member of a Trail Crew. The Buckeye Trail is divided into 26 sections, each with a Section Supervisor. The Section Supervisor oversees his/her assigned section and directs the work of Trail Maintainers/Adopters. Perhaps you live near the Buckeye Trail or have a special place on the Buckeye Trail you like to visit? Trail volunteers maintain at least a mile of the trail by keeping it clear of vegetation and painted with blue blazes so that hikers can find their way around Ohio. Trail work crews undertake bigger tasks by spending up to five days at a time working to build, repair, or tackle heavy maintenance issues. Since its inception in 1959, the BTA has grown into one of the largest outdoor volunteer networks in the state. Even with some paid staff support, the BTA is primarily driven by volunteer leadership.

Not an outdoors person, but have talent or experience in business, computers, law, resource management, social media, web design, advocacy, and/or program development, training? Are you good at organizing events? Raising money for non-profit organizations? These are the many ways to volunteer for the Buckeye Trail Association. Do you enjoy being in a leadership role? The BTA is searching for passionate, committed members for the Board of Trustees. Trustees represent the interest of BTA members from all over the state. They also work to raise money in order to improve, upgrade, promote, and make the Buckeye Trail a satisfying hiking experience.

Get discounts. Buckeye Trail Association members enjoy discounts on merchandise in the Buckeye Trail Shop, selected Ohio outfitters, and registration at larger BTA events. Also offered at a discounted rate are the Buckeye Trail maps. These 26 waterproof section maps include: a detailed point-to-point narrative of the trail; service listings such as camping, water, resupply; and points of interest. It's good to know that all proceeds go back into the mission of the BTA to build, maintain, promote and protect Ohio's 1,444 mile state trail.

The Buckeye Trail was chosen as Ohio's Millennium Legacy Trail in 2000, a national recognition of its historic importance and present-day value. Become a member and help protect an Ohio treasure.

www.buckeyetrail.org

Made in the USA
Middletown, DE
25 January 2020